THE
BIG DEAL
OF TAKING
SMALL STEPS
TO MOVE CLOSER
TO GOD

Also by
Bishop Vashti Murphy McKenzie

Journey to the Well

Not Without a Struggle

Strength in the Struggle

Swapping Housewives

Those Sisters Can Preach! (editor)

THE
BIG DEAL
OF TAKING
SMALL STEPS
TO MOVE CLOSER
TO GOD

Bishop Vashti Murphy McKenzie

Faith
Words

New York   Nashville

FaithWords
Hachette Book Group
1290 Avenue of the Americas, New York, NY 10104
faithwords.com
twitter.com/faithwords

First Edition: May 2017

FaithWords is a division of Hachette Book Group, Inc. The FaithWords name and logo are trademarks of Hachette Book Group, Inc.

The publisher is not responsible for websites (or their content) that are not owned by the publisher.

The Hachette Speakers Bureau provides a wide range of authors for speaking events. To find out more, go to www.hachettespeakersbureau.com or call (866) 376-6591.

Library of Congress Cataloging-in-Publication Data has been applied for.

ISBNs: 978-1-4555-9657-7 (hardcover); 978-1-4555-9655-3 (ebook)

Printed in the United States of America

LSC-C

10 9 8 7 6 5 4 3 2 1

To Vashti Gracia Murphy Saint Jean,
who gives me an opportunity to see the world
again as wonderment.

To the presiding elders, pastors, preachers, and
people of the Tenth Episcopal District of the African
Methodist Episcopal Church who grabbed
this vision and ran with it.

Contents

Take the First Step

Brothers and sisters, I do not consider myself yet to
have taken hold of it. But one thing I do: Forgetting
what is behind and straining toward what is ahead,
I press on toward the goal to win the prize for which
God has called me heavenward in Christ Jesus.

PHILIPPIANS 3:13–14 NIV

Discipleship isn't something you learn just by studying
it; at some point you have to do it.

KENDA CREASY DEAN

W<small>E</small> sent you up there to grow the people, not to kill them
off!" my presiding elder, the Reverend Edward P. Wilson, was
shouting over the telephone. My baptism into pastoral ministry
was not going well.

I had been assigned two churches in Chesapeake City, situated in the northeast corner of Maryland, a few miles away

from the Delaware and Pennsylvania state lines. When people asked where I served, I'd say, "In a place where if I sneezed, three states would respond with 'God bless you!'"

One was Ebenezer AME Church, a beautiful yellow church at the entrance of a prestigious horse farm, located between fields of ripening corn. The other was Bethel, a historic white-frame church in the city on the shores of the Chesapeake and Delaware Canal (also known to locals as the C and D Canal). On Sundays, passing ships invariably would blow their horns, strategically signaling the 11:00 a.m. worship hour.

There were seven members in my city church and a little more than two dozen in the second one. Three of the seven members at Bethel died within the first ninety days of my pastoral administration, leaving only four. Lord, help!

My presiding elder was eminently correct. I was sent to bring life and grow the people, but it just wasn't happening.

When you *grow* the people, you *grow* the church and *grow* the community. Rather than increase, death met me at the door. How was I going to help people grow when half of one church had already died?

How does one person serve as a channel and a catalyst for growth? It is a question I wrestled with during my season with the two congregations in Cecil County, Maryland, and subsequently at Oak Street and Payne Memorial AME churches in Baltimore. The Lord blessed my ministry in often extraordinary and miraculous ways in all four rural and urban congregations—Payne Memorial grew from my original three hundred members on roll in the early 1980s to more than seventeen hundred members before I became the 117th elected and consecrated bishop of the AME Church in 2000.

Nevertheless, the question is as relevant today as it was with my first seven members in Cecil County. I still wrestle with how to help people to grow in my current assignment as the presiding bishop of the Tenth Episcopal District of the AME Church, encompassing the state of Texas, with 202 churches.

I still hear Reverend Wilson's voice reverberating in the recesses of my memory: "We sent you to grow the people..." What I didn't realize was that as Reverend Wilson was challenging me to grow the people, God was challenging me to grow as a preacher, pastor, and person. As I swam the unfamiliar waters of pastoral leadership, God was cultivating the ground of my discipleship. I began to engage more intense and intentional means of growing closer to Christ to discern his will for me and for the people whom I had been charged to lead, the ones already present and the ones to come.

What began as my less than spectacular entry into pastoral leadership set me on a path that has led to my consistent desire to follow Christ as a servant and as a servant leader. I've taken a lot of small steps along the journey.

I believe the path to following Christ will evolve within each person who intends to experience new life by following the commandments of God and walking henceforth in God's holy ways, drawing near with faith. Once we give our lives to Jesus Christ, we want to be fully grown, mature Christians! We want to be grown enough to rightly handle the word of Truth (see 2 Timothy 2:15) and any circumstances, positive or negative, that come our way. We want to immediately know and understand God's will and purpose for our lives so we can live the abundant life Christ died to give us. We want this without realizing that every living creature grows gradually every day until fully matured, and that includes born-again believers.

Taking small steps becomes a big deal when you take the right steps that lead to major change in your life. A luxury car without an engine may look good on the outside, but it can't take you anywhere. Knowing the order of service and a few "church" words may sound good, but it won't take you very far.

If you've ever used stepping-stones to navigate a path in a garden or a rocky piece of land, then you know they help to make your footsteps certain and sure. Stepping-stones are small, so you can make a single step at a time and not be overwhelmed by the elements around you. Faith steps also can be small and deliberate, just like they are on the stones. And just as a landscaper intentionally places stones in certain places and spaces them accordingly, God orders our steps to keep us on a guided path to the places God intends for us (see Psalms 37:23; 119:133). God will make your feet like hinds' feet to walk on high places. The terrain is more challenging, but with feet like a sure-footed mountain deer, you will get to a new level of living (see Psalm 18:33).

Take a Step Forward

I was concerned about growing the church and growing the members in their discipleship. And, after my conversation with the presiding elder, I was especially concerned about the church growing.

I had a talk with God about it, and God revealed to me so much more than I could see with my limited human understanding.

God showed me that what I wanted for my churches was what God wanted for me: Let go of the process and trust God for the change you're praying for. God helped me to understand that change is a process, not an event, and that Jesus is the change agent. Movement from one experience to the next characterizes it.

The call to preach and pastor includes, for me, a responsibility to help draw the best out of others and myself along the way. Every time I'm privileged to preach; or teach a class, workshop, or seminar; or write a blog, podcast, or book, I am positioned to assist in whatever way God acts in the lives of those who hear or read my words.

While I operate in that call, I recognize that I am not stepping into the place of God. Rather, fulfilling my call means honoring the sovereignty of God as God operates in the lives that I touch in their various seasons of growth. Working in partnership with God to help people draw out all that God has placed in them means asking God, "How can I get into the flow of what you're doing so I can help others get to what you have placed in them?" It means I must first get into position through the spiritual disciplines of prayer, Word, worship, study, giving, testimony, service, and healthy living that can lead to more faith in God's power than in my own.

It is exciting to participate in birthing the dreams and visions of other people. "Jesus is just like having a baby," said one of my new members of the Chesapeake City Circuit. My face pushed my eyebrows up into my forehead. I waited for her punch line.

"Babies need love, attention, and a lot of stuff!"

I understood the "love and attention" part—that God loved us enough to give us God's Son, Jesus, and that we are to love the Lord with all of our heart, soul, mind, and strength. The "stuff" part puzzled me.

When I asked her about what stuff she was referring to, she responded that babies need a lot—car seats, high chairs, cribs, bottles, formula, day care, and safety gates.

"And Jesus?" I pushed further.

"With Jesus it's a new study Bible, Bible study, new members' class, prayer meeting, discipleship class, small-group ministry, tithes, offerings, and church every Sunday," she said with a bit of shock and awe in her voice. "Jesus gets all my love and the church demands all of my attention."

My new member had grabbed the gospel message with one hand and with the other hand held on to her social training. She believed that her old self was deleted and her new self was uploaded by faith through grace.

God deleted brokenness, pride, avarice, selfishness, low self-esteem, shame, abuse, depression, addiction, and hatred with the push of a button. These hindrances would no longer be a stumbling block. God uploaded boatloads of love, peace, joy, purity, mercy, and grace.

The virus that infected her spiritual computer was gone. Her life purpose was no longer compromised by inferior and evil software. At the same time she also believed that she had to handle the stuff that came along with the salvation package. If she got the right equipment, attended the right program, paid the right amount of money, and participated at the right level, she would live a life pleasing to God.

If she did all these things, she'd take a quantum leap from spiritual infancy to maturity, salvation to sanctification overnight. I prayed she wouldn't panic and go back to her old life. As Paul and Barnabas circled back around to strengthen the churches they had planted, I would have to keep circling back with her to provide opportunities for her to grow and mature in her new life in Jesus Christ (see Acts 14). It takes more than gathering data to replace panic with perseverance!

Follow Christ on Purpose All the Way

Moving closer to God is more than the accumulation of knowledge or participation in a program. We are saved by grace through faith in Jesus Christ not by keeping the Law or doing good works. Discipleship is a faith journey that takes a lifetime. It's a marathon, not a hundred-yard dash to the finish line of sanctification.

Rarely does anything major happen overnight. It may appear that an idea, a concept, an artist, a business, or a fashion arrives suddenly into the cultural spotlight. We tag it as an overnight sensation. Most of the time those things were developing in a place off our radar screen. We just didn't see it until it went viral on the Internet, made the talk show rounds where everyone saw it, or was repeated a nauseating number of times on the local and national news programs.

In our spiritual lives, change seldom happens suddenly. Deep down inside us, God is influencing our decisions or confronting our "dark night of the soul." God begins a conversation way off the radar screen of our consciousness. When we finally respond affirmatively to a life in Jesus Christ, it seems like it just happened overnight. But the process started like drops of rainwater seeping through the walls of an underground cave, causing minerals and other materials to grow into stalagmites from the ground up. God moves incrementally, a drop of love at a time, until we can no longer ignore the growth of grace in our hearts. A new divine reality is emerging. Every day we're given an opportunity to make choices that either enhance the growth of grace or hinder it.

As I prepared to deliver a sermon to hundreds of my peers, ministers of nearly every protestant denomination, at the Hampton Ministers' Conference, I considered the circuitous nature of my own growth in grace. As I waited my time to minister to the audience, I considered that there had been a few encouraging words offered when this city girl was assigned to two rural churches. There were also more than a few discouraging words. Everyone, it seemed, had an opinion about the direction my ministry should take. I should wait until a larger assignment became available, since I was a college graduate in seminary. I should wait for an opportunity closer to my home in Baltimore.

But I had prayed for *this* opportunity!

Early in my ministry, I had been invited practically every Sunday to be a guest preacher in different churches. But I longed to preach in the same place and partner with God in a ministry of reconciliation and transformation. "Lord," I petitioned, "give me a pastoral ministry that reconciles people to God and to each other, a ministry that transforms people who transform churches and communities."

I knew that changed people change the atmosphere of their environment, whether it is a home, a job, a church, or a community. God answered my prayer. As humble as my first assignment was, I was eager to begin, because I knew that a God-ordained assignment beats a human assignment every day, just like a God idea is always better than your good idea!

Our journey of discipleship is rooted in change. It is the only constant, the fact that nothing stays the same, including us. Since the time when Jesus called his first disciples from their fishing boat business, he has challenged those who would follow him to a higher level of living and relating to others. Those of us who accept that call submit to a spiritual journey that molds and shapes us to love the unlovable, to foster peace among the discordant, to help the helpless, and to seek justice for the oppressed.

Jesus inspired people to move out of their religious comfort zone to discover the power that comes from establishing a direct and personal relationship to God. He tore down barriers and built up the downtrodden. Everyone who encountered Jesus was dealt a faith challenge. Some despised him for it. But many, many more have accepted Christ as Savior and Lord and made the choice to follow him.

Most of us want to grow and experience Christ more deeply and fully. Everywhere I go, there are believers seeking. "I do all of those things, but I still feel like something is missing and I want to know what that is. I'm willing to pursue, investigate, change, grow, put down, pick up, set aside, or do whatever is needed to have the kind of deep and impactful relationship to Christ that he shared with Peter, James, and John." Thank God there are those who are still willing and wanting to strengthen their discipleship walk. Those believers want a path of intentional discipleship.

"I almost didn't make it," said my new member of the Chesapeake City Circuit. Her closest friends had a hard time accepting the fact that she'd made a decision to live a life pleasing to God. They didn't make it easy for her after her conversion. She was excited about Jesus and the stuff that came with the salvation package. Yet her friends kept tempting her to make choices that didn't support her new faith in Christ Jesus. "Sometimes I didn't do the right thing, and was hoping God wouldn't give up on me," she said.

Isn't it powerful to know that God will not give up on us? Jesus went back after his resurrection and called together his disciples, because he knew that even though they looked like a cowardly bunch in the aftermath of the crucifixion, the eleven remaining in his inner circle still had potential.

God sees in us what no one else can, and God patiently and consistently kneads it out of our spirit as we yield in obedience. Yielding is the newlywed husband who starts attending church with his wife simply to keep the honeymoon going. He might start off working the parking lot ministry because he can still stand outside and smoke. As he continues in his service and builds relationships with the pastor and other members, he moves from the parking lot to coaching the boys' Little League team. When the season ends, he gets recruited to serve in the male chorus and the usher board. He becomes convinced about the health hazards of smoking and asks for prayer to help him quit, then he does. Eventually, the man is invested in the life of the church to please Christ rather than his wife. Over time, his consistent service moves the pastor to enlist him for training to become a deacon or steward of the church. That describes the growth process of a believer who eventually decides on a path of intentional followship.

Better, Not Perfect

The commitment to moving closer to God does not mean perfection. The point is not to grow into a perfect follower, because no human being is perfect. But surely you resonate with the desire to be better. Media magnate Oprah Winfrey often credits the late Maya Angelou for teaching her a great lesson: "When you know better, you do better."

You want to do better. You want to understand better. You want to live better. You want to think better. You want to serve God better. You want to avoid temptation better. You want to let go of negative behaviors and increase positive ones. You want to expand your circle of friends living in obedience to Christ and narrow your association with people who drain your energy and emotions. You want to manage your finances better so you can give back to God, save for future and unexpected expenses, and bless your family. It's only human to want these things.

How will we get to a better place in our discipleship without being overwhelmed by the magnitude of the problems? Trying to solve all our issues at once is like auditioning for the role of Super Christian. Walking around with a big *C* on your chest can be a heavy burden, though, and it would take more strength than you have to hold that weight up on your own. God has not designed us so that we would solve all of our problems at once, then live happily ever after, free of trials and challenges.

We learn to cope with our problems through the experiences life presents to us. This means taking small but meaningful steps that collectively evolve into a big deal. Then, the problems that confront us today don't rattle us like they would have ten years ago, because we've been through enough to know that God will provide, that God will make a way, and that God will hide us in the time of trouble, equip us to get through it, or give us the strength to endure.

Nehemiah wanted to make life better for his kinsmen in his beloved city of Jerusalem (see Nehemiah 1), although the Israelites were living under Persian rule and authority. Nehemiah prayed and then chose to facilitate an incremental change by doing what he could do. Repairing their city's walls was the first priority that eventually led to revival (see Nehemiah 8). Nehemiah couldn't fix all of his people's problems, but he could fix the wall.

Like Nehemiah, even in your manageable steps you will encounter forms of opposition—whether deliberate or vicissitudinous. When living life better becomes the goal rather than living life perfectly, we can strive for improvements in a manner that is reasonable and consistent, and that we actually can accomplish.

Every believer who desires to be transformed can be. Transformation happens, as Paul admonished, "by the renewing of your mind" (Rom. 12:2 NIV). Change your mind; change your life.

The process of change is seldom immediate; rather, it is most often a protracted process of growth. At one season of life, we may grow most in Bible study. At other times, we are growing in our prayer life, and then in our giving. Through Bible study and prayer we may become convinced to give greater service and to take better care of ourselves.

Transformation comes through progression, which inspired the premise behind a small-step approach.

The call of discipleship in Jesus Christ is high and unwavering. Methodist icon Charles Wesley was so deeply moved regarding the immense command to be a follower of Jesus, he was inspired to write "A Charge to Keep I Have," which has been a core hymn of the church since the 1700s. Those of us who grew up in the Methodist tradition heard it time and again, whether or not we understood its meaning.

The second verse addresses our call to serve others:

To serve the present age,
My calling to fulfill:
O may it all my powers engage
To do my Master's will!

Over three hundred years ago, Wesley penned these words, having been inspired by the writings a century prior of theologian Matthew Henry:

We have every one of us a charge to keep, an eternal God to glorify, an immortal soul to provide for, needful duty to be done, our generation to serve; and it must be our daily care to keep this charge, for it is the charge of the Lord our Master, who will shortly call us to an account about it.

Our Savior has given us a job to do. And, as Henry asserted, God desires that we give our call everything that we can.

Yes, but How?

"I know what I want but I don't know how to get it," said Derrick while holding tightly to his wife's hand.

"And if it requires time or money, we can't afford it!" his wife, Kimlah, chimed in.

They were longtime members of one of the congregations I pastored in Baltimore. They'd been in church since children; however, they were churched but not changed.

Derrick was excited about a renewed relationship with Jesus Christ, but Kimlah couldn't see how they could add another thing to an already overloaded life. They each had two jobs to support their two children, two private schools with tuition and tons of extracurricular activities for both, two cars, one dog, and the big house of their dreams.

It was a Garden of Gethsemane moment (see Matthew 26:36–46). Jesus was amazed that his disciples couldn't pray with him for one hour. I was amazed at two people who'd invested so much time, talent, and energy in their children and material possessions and couldn't spare time to invest in a relationship with the Salvation of the World!

They were a great couple, very focused on taking the right steps toward having a good life for their family. Yet they seemed disinterested in taking steps to enhance the spiritual growth and development of that family. It's wonderful when we can provide the best life has to offer for our children and ourselves. Life doesn't stop there. God calls us to be courageous and put this life in perspective. Their focus reminded me of Jesus' Sermon on the Mount:

> Do not store up for yourselves treasures on earth, where moths and vermin destroy, and where thieves break in and steal. But store up for yourselves treasures in heaven, where moths and vermin do not destroy, and where thieves do not break in and steal. For where your treasure is, there your heart will be also... But seek first his kingdom and his righteousness, and all these things will be given to you as well. (Matt. 6:19–21, 33 NIV)

We desire to honor the responsibility of our call and are eager to please God with our Christian service. We may not know where to begin or how to find the time to do it. We need a strategy for obedience to God and emulating Christ on purpose rather than by merely stumbling upon a strong faith.

How can you give God your all when most of the time it seems like you don't have anything left to give?

In your quest to follow Christ and respond to the high call of your faith, the temptation is to try and confront every challenge and serve every need at the same time, but such attempts will only leave you exhausted and exasperated.

The challenge to serve can feel overwhelming at times. Jesus' twelve disciples had their own experience with the stress of life. They felt they had demonstrated their concern by reminding Jesus that it was time to take a break so the people could go and eat. Jesus would not allow them to dismiss the crowd's hunger. Imagine their shock at Jesus' command: "*You* give them something to eat" (Mark 6:37 NIV, emphasis added).

"What?!" Surely Peter, if not the others, must have thought, "He must be insane! How are we going to feed all of those people? We don't have that kind of money!" In addition to any logistical concerns they may have had, they informed Jesus it would take eight months' worth of their wages to feed all of those people. These men were overwhelmed by the task they were given in their call to follow Christ.

You may feel crushed by the weight of life's demands, including the "stuff" that comes with discipleship. Situations seem far too great for you to resolve. Thinking in human terms, thirteen men of ordinary means could not possibly have fed more than five thousand people. The Twelve did not see a way to feed all of those people, so they wanted to send them away, literally, every man for himself and his family. They wanted to shut down the challenge by dismissing the crowd rather than to take it on.

God may give you a task that causes your heart to flutter and your mind to respond, "Lord, do you know what you're asking me to do?" You may try to shut the call down if it seems too consuming. You may even try to reason with God: "Lord, how can I start a women's ministry when I'm raising our two children and my husband is stationed overseas for the next eighteen months?"

God's call always demands more of us than we think possible. Moses was overwhelmed by God's call (see Exodus 3) and gave excuses to the Lord at the burning bush. God's angel called to Gideon as the ironic "mighty man of valor" (Judg. 6:12 ESV) while he hid from the Midianites. Elijah hid in a cave after performing the greatest miracle of his ministry, because he was overwhelmed by Jezebel's threat to do him in (see 1 Kings 19:1–10). Jonah contemplated his fate in the belly of a big fish, overwhelmed by God's call to minister to a group of people he thought beneath him (see Jonah 1–2). Peter was overwhelmed by the accusation of being a Jesus follower and cursed at the Roman soldier to assert his innocence (see John 18:15–27).

The call to follow Christ and to serve usually comes in a way we have not conceived. God calls us out of our comfort zone. And even when we have a sincere desire to honor that divine summons, we may feel hindered by the real-world responsibilities of family, job, bills, and other obligations.

You want to obey God, but where do you start? The demands of living, breathing, and working, discovering your divine purpose, and finding your covenant partner are sometimes overwhelming. The job you thought was an answer to all your economic problems is creating more of them. Fear is killing your relationships. Temptation has you on speed dial. Shame is the name of the game, and you've scored a lot of points. Self-sabotage sends you back to a detrimental past, and you keep tripping over the same sins and negative people.

Daily pressures stress out our faith and bog down our minds. Anxiety sneaks up on us, and the energy needed to triumph is depleted far too quickly.

Your faith challenges you to care about those beyond your individual needs and beyond your circle of comfort. The youth ministry needs tutors. The children's ministry needs someone to form a praise dance troupe. Elderly church members need someone to check on them. There are many ways you can be a blessing to those closest to you and those you do not know who are members of your church or community. Jesus not only challenges you to care about the anonymous "them," but also to do something about the problems they face.

So, how do you follow Christ and serve humanity without feeling perpetually overwhelmed? After all, Jesus said in Matthew 11:28, "Come unto me, . . . and I will give you rest" (KJV), not "I will give you stress"!

You have the call to complete your God-assigned tasks, those special tasks that God calls you to—you know, the ones that God created for you and only you to do. And God equips and empowers you for these assignments. There are also spiritual disciplines that enhance and strengthen discipleship every day, practices available to every follower of Christ for any task: prayer, worship, praise, study, giving, service, sharing, learning, teaching. We're always looking for a new revelation when we haven't been doing what we're already empowered to do.

It seems like a lot when you try to blend your Christian duties into the recipe of your daily living. Growing in grace through the practice of discipleship means being consistent in taking the small steps of faith that lead to big changes in your life. Small steps keep your devotion and service to Christ fresh without being overwhelmed.

Most Christians try to get in a little prayer and a little giving back to the community. Maybe it dawns on you that you haven't been in communication with God as often as you should. You've missed a few Sundays at church because of work responsibilities, or you just wanted to chill out at home. Does the cover of your Bible have a fine layer of dust because you haven't studied the Word in a while? Yet you feel drawn to a deeper spiritual life?

Or are you at church so many times each week that home seems neglected? Is your calendar overbooked with church programs and projects and busywork?

You can move closer to God, because the baby steps that may seem insignificant at first can lead to great strides. Minor adjustments in your habits or routines often result in major benefits. Minute changes can chart the path to transformation.

Our faith in God can extricate us from living a "one-step-forward-and-two-steps-backward" lifestyle. And you can live a servant life without feeling perpetually overwhelmed.

Never Stop Growing

In the journey of life we must never stop growing. Paul wrote in the Bible that he had learned how to be content whatever his circumstances (see Philippians 4:11). That's a good lesson. You can be content with where you are or with what you have, but you must never be content to be what you are. Personal growth, which includes spiritual development, is like an escalator. You're either going up or going down, but you never stand still for any extended period of time.

Every Christian can stand a little more growth, no matter how long we've been on the walk of faith. Even the Apostle Paul wrote in Philippians 3:13–14 that he did not consider himself to have taken hold of everything, but he continued pressing toward the goal. In what areas of your life have you seen measurable growth? Where are you frustrated? Where do you need to take deliberate action to grow in Christ?

The big deal about small steps means taking seemingly little but purposeful steps that lead to big change. A step-by-step process to strengthen you as a follower of Christ brings big results. This plan is a means to a healthier spiritual lifestyle and a stronger growing faith. It enhances who you are and whom you are becoming.

You can grow when you initiate change in manageable

increments—a 10 percent increase in positive actions, or even a 10 percent decrease in negative behaviors. It's easier to initiate and a simpler discipline to maintain 10 percent changes. Plus, if you mess up, it is easier to start all over again!

For example, if you're praying about two minutes daily, you can begin the challenge by adding twelve seconds more to your prayer life. Once the additional seconds are solidly a part of your prayer routine, try to increase that by an additional 10 percent.

Twelve seconds seems doable right now, doesn't it? You're probably not stressed at the thought of adding a few more moments of prayer daily. You're thinking, "I can do that," so you already understand the challenge.

You may include opening words of praise and worship in your current prayer ritual, as I did in this model prayer:

> *God, I praise you as the Creator of all things great and small. I honor you as the God for whom nothing is impossible.*
>
> *Thank you, dear Lord, for allowing me to rise another day, for I know that it was you, and not my alarm clock, that awakened me this morning. I thank you for granting me health and strength this morning—my mind thinking clearly, my body functioning properly, and my heart desiring to spend time with you before my day begins.*
>
> *God, I pray for the physical endurance to keep up with the demands of today. May your grace and wisdom cover me during business hours. Grant me the presence of mind to lead the staff meeting with a servant's heart, seeking*

solutions rather than blame. As I encounter each of my coworkers today, Lord, let me show them the love of Christ. I pray that in all my actions I will show that I am your child. In my work, may I be a good example of Christian stewardship in the workplace.

Keep my mind clear and focused on all I need to accomplish today. Keep my family in perfect peace today, I pray. Bless the people I love in their workplaces today. Give them strength to rise above the pettiness in their workplaces. Lord, I pray that they will be granted the promotions that they deserve and that they have worked so hard for.

Protect children while they learn in school. Keep their minds focused on their schoolwork. Bless their teachers and give them a right heart to share knowledge with all the young ones in their charge. Be a hedge of protection around them throughout their day and keep them safe.

Lord, I pray for the family next door and any family experiencing struggle. Strengthen marriage, God, so couples can walk this journey together. I pray that their bond will deepen because of what they are having to endure right now.

Lord, bless our uprising and downsitting; our outgoing and our coming in. Empower us to stare down the impossible and scale mountains of challenge victoriously. Keep us away from those who can ruin our lives and surround us with those who affirm a life in Jesus Christ.

Forgive me, please, for my sins, done by commission and omission. May today be a better day so that I do not repeat the same mistakes.

An extension of your prayer may include more specific ways that you strive to grow and do better:

> *Today, Lord, guide me to be a more attentive friend and spouse and a more loving parent. Help me to remember that family is more important than work and people are more important than things. Help me to maintain a right order in my relationships—always putting you first. Help me to be a person whom my family views as honorable, and whom others will respect and regard with pride.*

The extra few seconds of prayer will not rob you of a significant amount of time, yet you will have extended the range of your prayer and increased your awareness of areas in your life that you need to address prayerfully.

The beauty of having a strategy for following Christ with intention is that it provides a way for you to be the better disciple you want to be in the way that you can do it most effectively. You can increase your praise and worship and your service to the community, your Bible study time, and your amount of time in corporate worship in manageable increments.

If you're just beginning your prayer life or your personal Bible study, start with ten minutes, or even ten seconds, then increase it 10 percent at a time. One step at a time, you can move toward sustained success. As you celebrate one small success, you'll be encouraged to go for more.

Our culture is fast, but very often change is not. The life transformations we seek result most often from slow and gradual practice. Your sincere discipleship is the steady, consistent, and intentional progress of the tortoise in a rabbit race of living. The tortoise wins and so will you!

Lasting Growth Comes Slowly

Incremental change is not always exciting, or even noticeable. Yet the big changes we often seek are rarely more than flashes in the pan. They are exciting and they get a lot of attention, but they do not always have the capacity to yield lasting change. Only you and the Lord will know that you've added twelve seconds of specific commitment to your daily prayer. But that can inspire you to continue adding 10 percent more until you have reached your personal prayer goal. As you continue adding to your prayer life or some other area of spiritual growth, your strength will increase to continue on the journey.

This small-step approach can be the vehicle for achievement in many areas of your life. You establish a manageable plan to follow, which is your set of directions on what to do, when to do it, and how to do it. This helps you prioritize what is truly important to you and eliminate the things you need to leave on the sideline—things and people who weigh you down, impede your progress, wear you out, frazzle your nerves, and get in the way of your earnest desire to be a strong follower of Christ.

Having a manageable strategy organizes the complex ingredients of your life so you can optimize resources and execute goals in increments. Accentuate your strengths and minimize your weaknesses, and be the vehicle for achievement in many areas of your life, because Christ is concerned about every area that affects you.

Discipleship is personal, practical, private, and public. The spiritual disciplines you practice in private will manifest themselves in public action. The personal internal steps you take will have an outward expression of action and activity that indicates change has taken place.

God draws us as learners or disciples to prayer and study and also to service. While we are praying, meditating, fasting, and feasting on the Word of God, we are engaged in the tools that prepare us to "go ye therefore…," as the Great Commission commands. Disciples are not meant to serve God in isolation. We come together in communities of faith to engage in acts of worship and service. "You've come to worship, now leave to serve" (John Wesley).

Serve This Present Age

Every generation within the Body of Christ must reach for the higher calling of discipleship. The issues facing "the present age," about which John Wesley wrote, vary depending on what we are called to do in service to Christ. In the 1950s and 1960s, serving the present age for many churches meant engaging in the fight for civil rights. For another generation, service may include medical missions or environmental or economic justice or literacy. But a church is trained to be the church only as individual believers equip and avail themselves of the tools for growing in faith and followship. "The scenery may change, over time," said Dr. Samuel DeWitt Proctor, "but the human condition remains the same."

When our third child made her entrance into the world rather suddenly the morning of Women's Day at Bethel AME Church in Chesapeake City, Maryland, my church community excitedly participated. The senior women had correctly predicted that this child would arrive the second Sunday in October. They said she would be a big baby, and thus not a quick delivery. They were certain that I had time to make it to my hospital in Baltimore. She wouldn't be born along the side of the road as we traveled back, nor would we need to detour to the nearest hospital in Christiana, Delaware. They believed that since she was a Sunday child, she'd be loving, giving, and happy. They were correct, but they missed the toddler phase when she stood up on the last pew on Sunday and shouted, as the choir ended its first selection, "I want it all and I want it right now!"

She was talking about her after-church snack, but for the rest of us, our shout may be for peace of mind, forgiveness, joy, financial security, emotional stability, the favor of God, or a fresh, new beginning. We want it all, and we want it right now.

My wise mother, Ida, gently leaned over to our third-born and gave her the "eye." You know that stern "I ain't having that in here" eye that has the power to stop a raging elephant and a toddler's tantrum. She then said, "You can have it all, but you can't have it all now."

What my mother told our toddler is true for growing in Christ. You can have it all, but you cannot have it all right now. Take the small steps. Eat this elephant one bite at a time. In the end, those small steps will add up to big changes in your spiritual life. Now, that's a big deal!

I offer this book to you as a guide to grow and develop a healthier spiritual lifestyle by taking small steps that lead to big change. Each chapter will focus on a strategic area of growth. Pace yourself. Go as fast or as slow as you need to through the book. It's up to you. It all begins with making a divine prayer connection and concludes with making an impact in the life and ministry of a congregation or community.

STEPPING-STONES

1. Think about your journey of discipleship and draw a line on a sheet of paper to represent your faith walk. Your journey will likely include highs and lows, loops, and returns to previous places. Write down the circumstances that caused low places and the joyous conditions that resulted in the high places. As you look back, how were the highs and lows connected? Would you have been able to experience the highs without the lows you incurred?

2. List the ways you have tried to change certain aspects of your life. Review the list and meditate on these words: Let go of the process of change and trust God for the change you've prayed for. Pray and affirm to God that you will yield your spirit to the process of change and allow Jesus to be the change agent in your life.

3. Are you struggling with something God has called you to do? Write a few paragraphs about what your life would look like if you were to answer yes to the life to which God has called you and get into the flow of what God is doing.

4. You likely have prayed for certain opportunities to manifest in your life—job, home, children, spouse, health, etc. Pray about opportunities for spiritual growth so that you may be more equipped as a disciple.

5. Most people strive to have a better life. What steps do you believe you need to take to become a better follower of Christ? Consider the other areas of your life that would be affected by greater discipleship and service—home, family, work, community, relationships, etc.

6. Read the lyrics to "A Charge to Keep I Have," and apply them to your own life. What does it mean for you to "serve this present age" as a follower of Jesus Christ?

Connect

Pray without ceasing.

1 THESSALONIANS 5:17 KJV

We are all inextricably connected to each other by a power greater than all of us, and...our connection to that power and to one another is grounded in love and compassion.

BRENÉ BROWN, *The Gifts of Imperfection*

On a Palestinian expedition with a group of women bishops in the Methodist tradition, we visited an economic cooperative between a group of Israeli and Palestinian women. They all lived across the road from each other along the rolling countryside outside of Bethlehem. These women were separated only by borders of religion and culture. The Israeli women were faring better economically, and they decided they could help their Palestinian neighbors by creating a market for their creative expressions, like weaving baskets that were functional works of art.

One of the Israeli women shared with us the importance of being connected amid such religious and political volatility. It was critical that they remained connected to their husbands and families via their mobile phones in case of sudden violence or hostilities elsewhere. They needed to know if and where there was trouble and if they needed to get to safety. It was equally important for them to stay in communication to know that their loved ones were alive and safe.

One day, violence broke out. The Israeli husbands frantically called their wives immediately and asked their location. The women were across the road visiting their Palestinian neighbors. They were told to go home to safety. One of the wives refused. They were safe where they were. Their friends would see to their safety. Each group of women would look after the other.

Staying connected was essential to their survival. The women maintained communication with each other and their familial community via mobile phone. This sisterhood among women from two different cultures and religions represented a critical link. Equally important was the association of neighbors, which provided a sense of security during times of trouble. Connection is important.

Connection provided an energy that repurposed their behavior and actions beyond cultural and religious restrictions. Each group was seen, heard, and valued, and as such the groups were strengthened and sustained by that association.

Life is a series of connections. From infancy, we need association with others. Our early associations come primarily through touch. A century ago, babies deemed unwanted were placed in orphanages, and most of these infants died before they were a year old. Researchers have discovered that the high infant mortality rates within orphanages in the early twentieth century and before were strongly connected to the insufficient amount of human contact the babies received. Even when those babies were given the proper nutrition and care, they still did not receive adequate amounts of touch—connection—and so the majority of them stopped growing and eventually perished. Babies need to connect with other humans in their formative years, but our need to be linked to others does not end with infancy. Our need to form attachments beyond self continues throughout our lifetime.

Sociologists, psychologists, and neuroscientists have devoted a significant amount of research to the human need to make connections. In 1951, McGill University researchers conducted an experiment on sensory deprivation. A selected group of male graduate students were paid to stay in small, confined chambers equipped with only a bed. They could leave the space only to use the bathroom. The subjects wore goggles and earphones to limit their senses of sight and hearing. They also wore gloves to limit their sense of touch. The original research plan was to conduct the experiment for six weeks. None of the students lasted more than a week. Most of the student subjects experienced a diminished ability to think clearly, and others suffered hallucinations.

We all need to connect. Our human, relational connections are vital to our well-being. God created us to be connected to all of God's creation. We're hardwired to be connected to creation and to each other.

Our connection with God keeps us rooted and grounded for all of our other interpersonal relationships—marriage, friendship, family, professional, social, or community. We are positioned to have much healthier relationships when we have a stronger relationship with God.

Things can happen to disrupt our spiritual connection. People, places, and things can corrode our Holy Hookup, just like battery acid eats what links a car engine to its power source. There is also the "sin which so easily ensnares us" (Heb. 12:1 NKJV).

A number of times in my life the "ties that bind" might have been severed. My connection with God could have been severed when our baby died after a few hours of life, or when my mother suddenly died, or when an irreversible disease befell someone I loved dearly. Each of these events, however, became "But God" moments. I could have wallowed in self-pity—but God kept me in my right mind to remember that I had so many blessings there was no room in my life to feel sorry for myself (see Ephesians 3:20). Grief might have consumed me—but God gave me comfort and peace that flooded my soul and soothed my spirit (see Psalm 119:50, 76). I could have been overwhelmed with doubt—but God gave me renewed strength to stand and wait to see the goodness of the Lord (see Isaiah

41:10). I could have given up on conceiving another child after our newborn died—but God reminded me that God's mercies are new every day (see Lamentations 3:22–23). My sanity and my salvation depended upon staying connected to God.

How is your connection to God? Is the Almighty your "ride or die" or "ride and live" partner who goes with you through every circumstance? Or is your relationship to God more like that of a Facebook friend whose posts you see from time to time, occasionally giving a "Like" when something hits your spiritual radar?

We all can have a stronger connection to God, and there's a simple way to begin. God's people must pray. It's how we connect to God. It's how God's people have always made connections to God. Prayer is our way of being in the presence of our Creator. And prayer is incremental.

The Four *S*'s of the Small Steps of Connecting to God

We serve a God of decency and order, so it makes sense to approach our connection to God with the same protocol. Effective prayer means more than babbling words as part of a performance or a ritual to check prayer off your daily list of things to do.

Intentional prayer consists of elements that incrementally establish and maintain your connection to God. God always stands ready to connect to us, but distractions and misplaced priorities can interfere with our connection to God.

Solitude—Being Alone with God

But when you pray, go into your room, close the door and pray to your Father, who is unseen. Then your Father, who sees what is done in secret, will reward you.

MATTHEW 6:6 NIV

"I'm afraid of being alone with God!" blurted out one of my Circle of Love members. The Circle was a women's Bible fellowship that I started at both Oak Street and Payne Memorial when I served these congregations as their pastor. It was a bimonthly gathering to search for biblical answers to our daily crises and challenges. The Circle was a safe place to share our deepest thoughts without fear they would be repeated outside the group.

"I have no problem praying in the Circle or with someone else. It's when I sit quiet for a while, I'm afraid that God is going to say something or do something that will scare me to death," she shared.

"Try this," I responded. "Find your quiet space and set your watch...Today I would say set the stopwatch app on your phone to two minutes. Pray, ' "Speak, for your servant is listening" [1 Sam. 3:10 NIV]. Lord, say something or do something that will love me to life.' " Then just be still until the timer sounds."

Sacred solitude liberates us from the fear of being alone with God or ourselves. Building a strong prayer life calls for us to step away from the ordinary and the extraneous, to turn off the noise and everything with an on-off switch. It begins by taking advantage of the solitudes that are present every day. The early morning solitude in bed before the business of the day, or over a cup of tea or coffee in a quiet place, may help you to incrementally increase the quantity or quality of your prayer time. Find quiet moments in the tiny snatches of time in rush-hour traffic, or quiet places outside your home like a park, tree, patio, garage, or sanctuary.

The progression of time spent in prayer is important, no matter how small the increments. The next day set your stop-watch app to three, then four, five, ten minutes, and so on until you no longer need to set a timer. You're now comfortable alone in the presence of God.

I spent most of my summers at YMCA and Girl Scout camps. I loved being away from the hot concrete sidewalks and city life in the sweltering heat and humidity. At Camp Mohawk on the Patuxent River in Southern Maryland, I walked in the cool of the morning listening to the voice of God. In the cool of the night I watched the wonder of God in the Milky Way. The city lights wiped out this wonder of a trillion stars splashed across the sky, but alone in a sacred solitude, as I walked across the field between the cabins of the Cherokee and the Chippewa Nations, the stars spoke to me of the glory of God. Find your places of solitude and connect by being alone with God.

Submission—Putting Ourselves in the Hand of God

> *But the Advocate, the Holy Spirit, whom the Father will send in my name, will teach you all things and will remind you of everything I have said to you.*
>
> JOHN 14:26 NIV

Surrender and *submission* are negative words to many people. Yet, we surrender ourselves to circumstances beyond our control: dead-end jobs and negative supervisors. We surrender to popular opinion instead of developing our own, based on fact instead of stereotypes. We submit ourselves to relationships based on biological clocks instead of allowing God to be our relationship arranger.

Do something radical. Surrender to God, who knows your past, present, and future. Submit to a God who has your best interest at heart. "If you, then, . . . know how to give good gifts to your children, how much more will your Father in heaven give good gifts to those who ask him!" (Matt. 7:11 NIV). In prayer, strive to be yielded and still before God. Yield your body, mind, and soul to the Lord at the beginning of each day: "*Lord, whatever you want me to do, wherever you want me to go, whatever you want me to say, in whatever way you desire.*" It is the first thing you pray in the morning and the last thing you pray at night.

In the mystical moments of solitude we steal away to Jesus for ourselves. He speaks to us and we are humbled and open to hear the Lord and submit to divine instruction. We open ourselves to the plans that God has for us, which are always plans for our good and not to harm us.

In solitude, we connect to God in a most intimate manner. Through intentional quiet, we remove competition for our attention to God and establish an unfettered connection to the Almighty. When we still our thoughts and turn them toward God, we make ourselves available to God's Spirit, leading us to new revelations of God.

Service—Do What the Lord Commands

> *Only fear the* LORD, *and serve Him in truth with all your heart; for consider what great things He has done for you.*
>
> 1 SAMUEL 12:24 NKJV

From our tiny snatches of silence, solitude, and submission, we receive divine direction to look beyond ourselves to others. Often in the quietest moments, God reveals our greatest assignments. Go. Do. Touch. Now. In that secluded moment, we are ready to listen—without distraction. God is able to use us to be a blessing to those who are either closest to us or far away on the other side of the world.

When God speaks to us during those private moments, we go forward every day having been formed and transformed in prayer and nurtured by the Holy Spirit to a new awareness of

God's presence. We go forward with new assurances, joy, and peace as followers of Jesus Christ. We go forward putting feet to our prayers.

As hectic as life can be, it's time to stop, stand still, and hear what's on the Lord's agenda before we make out our own.

Selah—"Stop Here Before Moving Forward"

Selah is a word used in the Hebrew Bible, often in the book of Psalms, as a notation or direction to musicians or a choir. "Trust in Him at all times, you people; pour out your heart before Him; God is a refuge for us. *Selah*" (Ps. 62:8 NKJV, emphasis added). It can mean "stop and listen" or "those who have ears listen and those who have eyes see." *Selah* can also mean "stop here before moving forward."

Selah is our call to pause and hear, take in, reflect and consider. Listening is a major factor in our receiving information, along with understanding and comprehension.

Our ability to listen plays a major role in our gaining pleasure or displeasure from what we hear and learning from the information. We do it every day. We ought to be good at it! Nevertheless, research suggests we're not as good as we should be at listening. We remember only 25 to 50 percent of what we hear. If someone is talking for more than ten minutes, the listener is paying attention to less than half of the conversation.

Listening to God, like listening to other people, can be challenging. It's a conscious effort. You must desire to pay attention without getting bored or losing focus. The key to truly hearing someone is to listen first, without formulating your response, while the other person is talking. When you listen to God, don't assume you know what God's answer will be.

Listening is paramount. "A man prayed, and at first he thought that prayer was talking. But he became more and more quiet until in the end he realized that prayer is listening" (from Søren Kierkegaard, *Christian Discourses*, as quoted in Richard Foster's *Celebration of Discipline: The Path to Spiritual Growth*).

As you strive for a deeper connection with God, ask the Lord to help you prevent life's challenges from robbing you of the opportunity to listen to those around you, especially those you love, including God!

Take time to be silent each day, inviting the presence of God into your spirit. Get away to a place of solitude. Set your stopwatch app if you have to or just let the Lord be your guide. Put yourself into God's hands and in a posture of humility and submission to lose your life for Christ's sake (see Mark 8:35). This leads to service, doing what the Lord commands. Finally, *Selah*. Stop to connect with God through prayer before moving forward.

Is God Looking for You?

I started to miss my brand-new Bethel Chesapeake member. She didn't show up for two Tuesday night Bible studies, missed Friday night prayer meeting, and was missing in action in Sunday worship. I called her to find out if she and her family were all right.

"I slipped and fell," she responded. Did she go to the hospital? Was she under a doctor's care?

"No," she replied. She'd slipped in her walk with Christ and fell back into her old lifestyle. "I didn't think you'd notice my absence."

Oh, but I did. Her seat was empty. Her voice was missing. Her smile was not there to light up the room. I left the church wondering what happened and if I needed to go beyond phone calls to look for her. She was missing in action.

In the Garden of Eden, when Adam and Eve attempted to hide from their Creator, God went looking for them (see Genesis 3). When we get lost in daily minutiae, wander like stray sheep from the herd in hostile territory, or go away like a prodigal child, God will look for us (see Luke 15). God wants to connect with us.

When the twelve disciples scattered and went into hiding after the crucifixion of Jesus, the resurrected Christ found them (see John 20) to renew the connection they had shared during his earthly ministry.

God desires to spend time with us through prayer and meditation. Prayer is how we receive divine insight, direction, and correction. Moses prayed with his back to the past and his foot at the edge of the future. David prayed before going into battle. Jesus went apart to pray early in the morning in the midst of ministry mayhem.

Most believers will say they pray with some regularity. Intentional prayer is a consistent connection that can take several shapes and forms. Intentional prayer is an invitation to explore the many prayer models—not making a religion out of prayer, but rather responding to an invitation to connect beyond yourself to a greater power source.

This kind of prayer requires trust. You trust God to hear and respond. God must trust you to connect, listen, and respond even if the answer is unwanted.

Have Your Prayers Hit a Stained Glass Ceiling?

Julian, a frustrated prayer warrior, came to my office one day while I served as pastor at Payne Memorial. He had been praying for months for success in his career and all of the monetary perks that go with it. He prayed the Prayer of Jabez (see 1 Chronicles 4:9–10) to bless him indeed with a greater impact and an enlarged territory. He prayed John 3:2, that he would prosper and be in good health. As he prayed, he remembered that it was the Lord who gave him the ability to produce wealth (see Deuteronomy 8:18). But he was discouraged, because his prayers seemed to be going nowhere.

Many kinds of viruses can clog a connection to God and the answer to prayer. Some believers pray rightly, but with wrong motives. Unconfessed sin or requests contrary to the Word of God can hinder petitions. Evil can hold up an answer. Daniel prayed, but the angel with the answer was delayed twenty-one days because of evil opposition (see Daniel 10:10–14). You may offer the right prayer but at the wrong time. The answer to your prayer may be hindered because what is needed to bring the prayer to fruition is not ready or you're not ready.

Julian and I prayed together for clarity, and I suggested that he change the focus of his prayer. Instead of praying for what he wanted God to do, I suggested Julian let God know that he was available for whatever God wanted to do in his life. Julian changed his prayer: *"Open the doors of opportunity you want me to go through. Send me to those you want me to be a resource for, and give me the experiences you want me to have to prepare me for the future that you have in mind."* We also prayed that God would give Julian the peace necessary to trust God for the answers.

Whenever thoughts about his future flooded his mind, Julian prayed this same prayer. In due season, God opened doors in the areas he had studied in college but had long since forgotten. His résumé landed in front of decision makers who were willing to invest in his future. His breakthrough was not for his personal benefit alone, but also so he could be a conduit of blessings to others. Change didn't happen overnight. It happened over time.

How's your prayer life? Do you pray daily, or only when something goes wrong or you need divine intervention? We should keep our lines of communication open at all times. If you've ever had a friend or relative who calls only when he or she wants something, then you know it's not a pleasant feeling. God wants to have an ongoing, unbreakable connection with us, not just an every-now-and-then plea for help.

Prayer is two-way communication with God. That means talking as well as listening for God's response. When you pray, do you do all the talking, or do you make yourself available to hear what God wants to tell you? Your efforts to expand your relationship with God can include spending time in silence after you say amen and waiting for God to speak.

Expand the depth and breadth of your prayer life by keeping track of what God is doing in your life. Keep a prayer journal to record your petitions. Then write in your testimony after God has answered your prayer. Keeping a journal can encourage you while you wait for God to answer your current prayer. Reviewing what God has done in your life can remind you of what God is able to do in your life. Reading about your answered prayer will renew your faith; you will know that what God has done once, God is able to do again.

Wherever you are in your prayer life, take time to access how you can strengthen your communication with God, and then strive to improve in a way that won't cause you to feel defeated before you even begin.

God eagerly awaits our entry into the sacred place, under the shadow of the Almighty. We are invited to come to this place daily. The longer we dwell there, the more we learn how to depend upon God alone. In that place of solitude and connection, God will energize us and fill us with love, joy, and peace. When we begin the day in God's presence, that connection assures us that the day has been prepared for us with attention and great detail.

There's Power in Connecting to God

It is so easy to underestimate the supernatural power of prayer. In prayer, like meditation, we are growing into "a familiar friendship with Jesus," according to Thomas à Kempis (*Imitation of Christ*). The growing part is a learning opportunity that helps us when we are disillusioned by disappointments or when we regard prayer as unproductive, dismissing its power. We don't have to be experts in prayer. We must only be willing to learn. "Lord, teach us to pray" (Luke 11:1 NIV). Connecting to God links us with a Power who does not know what impossible looks like. When we pray, our determined connection to God becomes God's opportunity to intervene in our life and in the lives of those we care about.

Early in our marriage, my husband was working twelve-hour days and our son, John, was just a toddler. We needed divine intervention. I wanted to generate additional income for our family, but I also wanted to have hands-on time with our son. So I prayed. I connected to God in a different way, because it seemed that what I asked for was a bit outrageous. I asked God for a part-time job with a full-time salary!

Nevertheless, I engaged in this prayer. Not long after, I got an unexpected phone call from Dewey Hughes. "I want you to audition for this job. We're starting a contemporary gospel station in Washington, DC, called Message Music. You'll need to get an FCC license so you can handle the equipment." I went to the interview with Cathy L. Hughes, the first woman vice president and general manager at a radio station in Washington, DC. I knew virtually nothing about the business of radio programming—queuing music, operating the controls, or developing a playlist. Plus, I had to study hard to obtain my engineer's license. But I got the job!

My initial work hours were from 10:00 a.m. to 2:00 p.m., which gave me the flexibility I needed to still spend some of my day with our son. Just what I'd prayed for! Even more amazing, the pay was commensurate to a full-time salary! God answered my prayer in a miraculous way, but I had to do some things to bring God's answered prayer to fruition. I studied hard and learned the business of radio. Eventually, I was promoted from radio personality at midday drive time to afternoon drive time. From there, I was promoted to program director, then to operations manager, and finally to general manager at another radio station in Baltimore and on to corporate vice president of programming.

When I got the employment offer, I was astonished to be hired for a job I knew nothing about. But I know the position came about through prayer. Only God could have opened that door and orchestrated the sequence of events that followed. God paved the way, because I had connected to God through prayer. I learned through two radio stations, one in Washington and the other in Baltimore, that God will never put you in a position that you're not prepared for or willing to learn!

Stay connected to God for the major issues of life, but not only that. God wants to stay in touch with you on a daily basis. Start your day every day by strengthening your connection with God in prayer. God wants to enter into the lives of believers daily. Don't start your day without that conversation with the Lord. The challenges of this world are too great to handle alone. Seek God first and foremost, and then the pieces of your life will fall into place.

"Steal Away to Jesus"

Enslaved African Americans sang the words to this beloved Negro spiritual, implying on its surface that they were singing of a time when they would be with the Lord in heaven. The song's deeper meaning was in a cloaked language to communicate a late-night meeting to plan an escape or to worship. Their faith was not a panacea, but rather one of empowerment. They took the misinterpreted words of oppression and found God's word of liberation.

The daily life of an enslaved fieldworker, according to historians, consisted of work from sunup to sundown six days a week. They lived in harsh conditions, but they still found time to steal away to Jesus so they could connect with God.

If oppressed people made sacrifices and put themselves at personal risk in order to connect to God, what's your excuse? A career that gives you regularly scheduled times for breaks and lunch means a few available moments to steal away to Jesus. A home that provides safety and comfort is also a haven where you can arrange a few moments early in the morning or late at night to steal away to Jesus.

The busyness of our lives often necessitates that we steal away time to connect to the Source of our strength and power. It means carving out time to be still and quiet, a time for just you and God.

Many are afraid of being alone, like my Circle of Love member, even during times of connecting with God. They associate aloneness with loneliness, grief, and sadness. Recognize that you can be alone without being lonely or in a bad or negative space. Some fear

God's judgment in the quiet of aloneness. Some fear that God has no time for them. Others are afraid of the dark or have lived in untrustworthy environments where for safety's sake they had to anticipate disruption. The silent spaces could not be trusted. When your time alone with God becomes a connection rather than isolation, you cherish your time alone with God and do all you can to protect and preserve it. Being alone with God in quiet and tranquility can be a transformative experience. God can lead you through your present circumstance and on to something new.

Having meaningful personal encounters with God depends on cultivating an environment where conversation with God can be made a priority. Prayer involves both talking to God and listening, so you need a place where that can happen. When you position yourself to hear from God as well as speak, you open the door for God to move in you.

Sometimes you may have to connect with God amid a noisy or even raucous environment with prayers spoken in haste and urgency. Such prayers are essential and vital to the situation or the moment, but words of petition uttered quickly do not make for a full prayer life that builds a true connection with God.

Have you ever tried speaking to someone in a noisy environment, like at a football game or a concert? It's almost impossible to communicate effectively in those situations. You would never choose a noisy place to have an intimate, meaningful conversation, such as a discussion about marital issues or a family concern. The many distractions would render the conversation almost pointless. You would choose a different location that allowed you to focus on the matter at hand. You might have to talk about something quickly in a noisy environment, but only out of necessity. For instance, if your son got hurt playing in a football game, your spouse might come over to you and utter, "Our son is hurt. He's basically okay, but we need to go and see about him." But you wouldn't choose the football game setting to discuss your concern about your son's failing grade or your distrust of a new friend he's acquired. As responsible and caring parents, you would choose a time when you could be alone to discuss such an important family issue. Critical issues are wisely discussed in a place where they can be given the time and attention they merit.

Moses was alone with God at the burning bush. While Moses was tending to his father-in-law's flock, God caught his attention and summoned him via a burning bush (see Exodus 3). Imagine if Moses had been distracted by the chatter and laughter of his sisters-in-law had they accompanied him while he cared for the cattle. Could God have gotten his attention so readily? Moses was alone going about his daily routine when God drew him in.

Sometimes God allows us to be in a situation of isolation so that God's voice can be heard. Gideon was alone when God commissioned him to save Israel. Gideon's political circumstances positioned him to be alone when God called him. He hardly looked like the "mighty man of valor" (Judg. 6:12 ESV) that God saw in him. But as Gideon sat alone, he was able to hear the voice of God address him directly.

Esther purposely carved out time to be alone with God before going to see the king (see Esther 4). She was about to take an action that was quite daring, perhaps even dangerous. The young queen wisely prostrated herself before the Lord in fasting and prayer prior to making a move forward.

Peter was alone on the rooftop when God instructed him to go to the Gentiles. The Apostle's prejudices had impeded his mission to take the good news to all the world. God spoke and showed him the value of all God's creation (see Acts 10).

Jacob was the trickster who thought he had it all under control. In his younger years, he got what he wanted but lost what he needed the most. God wrestled Jacob's old life from him until the blessing of his new life was obtained (see Genesis 32). While Jacob was alone in his camp, God came to him in the night, and the two struggled until the break of dawn. Jacob was unwilling to let go of this pivotal and precious moment of alone time with God. He emerged a changed man, from whom God would continue building a great nation.

Once you recognize the power that lies in your intimate connection with God, you will treasure such moments as Jacob did. God is revealed as you engage in intimate communion through prayer and meditation. In prayer, God can show you visions for your future. In prayer, you can see a greater future for yourself, one that honors God and serves humanity. Your quiet time with God is God's invitation to speak to your heart, which has been prepared to listen.

I still vividly remember a Sunday fairly early in my pastorate when I had to steal away to Jesus. I waited until the church was empty, while my family busied themselves preparing to make the long drive from Chesapeake City to Baltimore. My husband was packing my "office" of hymnals, Bibles, AME *Discipline* books, extra bulletins, and Communion sets in the trunk of our car.

My mother was making sure that our toddler daughter and playful son had emptied their bladders and washed their hands before being strapped into their car seats. The church members—the four remaining of Bethel and the dozen or so who came to worship from Ebenezer—had gone home to their Sunday dinner, with one exception. Brother Nathaniel Brady, a faithful officer, stood outside the door of Bethel's one-room sanctuary. He didn't know it at the time, but he was standing guard.

I sat silently in the last row, six months into my first pastoral assignment. There were about six pews in the center section and an equal number of smaller ones on either side along the walls. In the back of the church on either side were restrooms. I hung my two robes, one black and one white, on a rack in the ladies' room, which doubled as my quiet "get-yourself-together-before-worship" space.

I sat in the last row and surrendered my preaching, pulpit, and pastoral ministry to Jesus. It is something that I have consistently and actively repeated at every episcopal and pastoral assignment. I surrender myself to the Lord at every insurmountable mountain and during every impossible situation. "It's not my will, but thy will be done."

In that moment, as Brother Brady stood guard, I talked to God: *"Lord, I know you have called me to do this. You have given me everything I need to be a blessing to this congregation and community. Use me to bring the Word of Life to all of the dead places in their lives. I surrender myself to you. I surrender my thought life, my heart, my soul, and my strength to you. I surrender my desires and dreams for my church, my family, and myself. I give what is already yours back to you—these two churches, officers, members, families, neighborhoods in Chesapeake City, and all the communities from the C and D Canal to Cecilton, Maryland. This is your church. Do what you want to do with your church. These are your people. Do what you want for your people. I place everything into your hands. Show me how to shepherd and instruct them. Give me your Word to preach. What service shall we render in this place? In Jesus' name, amen."*

Tears streamed down my face. I sat waiting. Listening. Finally I heard, "I will never leave you nor forsake you."

Jasmine, my not-yet-two-year-old, found her way into the church past Brother Brady. She climbed into my lap and gave her mother the hug she needed. She was too young to understand the tears but old enough to feel the emotion. This was the child who would later come down the aisle of another church a few years later, tears streaming down her own cheeks, to surrender her life to the Lord.

As my toddler quieted herself on my lap, I quieted myself in the presence of the Lord. Like David, with all of his goals, plans, and responsibilities as king and warrior, I—with all my roles and responsibilities—quieted myself as a child in the lap of a parent. *"Lord, my heart is not proud; my eyes are not haughty. I don't concern myself with matters too great or awesome for me. But I have stilled and quieted myself, just as a small child is quieted with its mother. Yes, like a small child is my soul within me.*" (See Psalm 131:1–2.)

The act of sitting on that pew quietly wasn't a lot, humanly speaking, but I now realize that I was making a huge step forward to God.

All the answers I was looking for didn't drop like manna from the sky. What I found was a peace that permeated my very being. The peace flooded my spirit, relentlessly tossing my self-sufficiency aside. All of my plans and ideas were thrown against the unforgiving shore of pride and performance.

The peace cascaded over my spiritual "to-do" list for the church. It broke up my agenda and washed away my organizational charts. It created space for God to work, removing the worry, fear, doubt, and stress. What was left was not a perfect pastoral plan, but rather a peace that said, "God is in charge." God returned, "You're looking for ways to grow the people. I'm looking to grow you."

I heard from God in the still of the sanctuary that day. You can prepare to hear from God by making room for God to enter your heart and mind. Let God dwell there and consume you with divine, holy presence. Get up five minutes early to hear from God. Go into a private space while everyone else in the house is watching television or otherwise occupied. You don't have to find hours of time; spending just a few moments a day with the Lord can change your life. Choose an amount of time—one minute, five minutes, ten or more—and then commit to that. The length of time is not as important as the consistency of your connection activity with God.

Beloved, I know how hard it is sometimes to make space in your life even for a few moments alone with God. My alone time is possible only because I get up early in the morning to steal away with Jesus. When our children were young, I treasured those quiet morning moments before the patter of little feet announced the day had begun. When I was working full-time, while simultaneously pastoring a church and enrolled in a seminary, my moments of solitude with God didn't come until late in the midnight hour. I made sacrifices to savor my special connections with God.

Your connections with God will depend on your life circumstances. Choose the time and space that works for your life, not someone else's! God has called us to God's best and highest. We must be willing to be alone with the Lord sometimes to hear what cannot be heard in the midst of our busy lives. Surrender your own idea of how things ought to be and lend yourself to God's voice and call.

You *Can* Find the Time!

Your small steps to a closer connection to God may call for an increase of quantity or of quality. You may not be spending a sufficient amount of time engaged in prayer. If the area you want to improve is your quantitative time connecting to

God, you can improve that via simple mathematics. If you are spending no time regularly in prayer, commit to giving thirty seconds. Is that it? Yes, for now. The important thing is to start somewhere and establish the discipline of prayer as part of your lifestyle. You can increase the amount of time you spend in prayer later. Now what's most needed is the routine of prayer.

If you don't know how or where to begin a deeper prayer life, try reading the Lord's Prayer (see Matthew 6:9–13) or reciting it from memory. As you continue to repeat the words, you likely will feel moved to add your own to make your prayers more personal.

Where can you find thirty seconds—or perhaps thirty more seconds—to spend in prayer? Maybe you can establish a routine of prayer before you turn the key in the ignition headed for work. You can pray while sitting in the car before you put the gear in Drive and take off for work. Maybe it's in the bathroom. If you're like I was when our children were young, the bathroom was often my place of solitude. Maybe it's the thirty seconds before you step into the shower. If you ride the bus or take the train to work, you may build the foundation of your prayer closet amid the anonymity of public transit. Wherever you find your momentary place of solace, take no less than thirty seconds and then keep building on the seconds. Seconds then grow into minutes, until you are no longer conscious of passing moments; you're prospering in the presence of God.

When you begin to see how a devoted prayer and meditation time improves your life, you will begin to guard your time with the Lord and protect it from intrusion.

When you honor your relationship with God through daily

prayer, you cultivate the foundation you need to create even more time and space for regular connections with God. Building a strong connection with God will help you live with confidence that God is able to do with you and for you according to God's Word and your faith.

How Do You Start Your Day?

"I don't feel like praying," said my third-born, Joi-Marie, weary of praying in the car on the way to Bethel Christian School with her older sister.

"Pray even if you don't feel like it," I responded. "Once you get started, your faith will cancel your 'not feeling like it.'"

She prayed. By the time she had prayed for her principal, Dr. Peggy Wall, teachers, classmates, and for God to bring to her remembrance of what she had read and studied at home, we were at school waiting on her to say, "In Jesus' name, amen!" She just needed to get started. It's like an old car (a hoopty) that needs a push to help get it started. Once the engine is engaged, it's ready to roll. Just get started. Crank up that prayer engine early, and you'll be ready to roll for the rest of your day.

Even the most faithful believers can slip away from the discipline of prayer. But for some Christians, spending time with God is not where they feel they are lacking. For these disciples, quality will be the focus of a move toward greater intentionality. While not necessarily quantifiable, striving for a deeper prayer life can be a worthwhile reason to step out of your spiritual comfort zone.

What is the first thing you do when morning opens the gateway to your conscious mind and you realize that the grace of God has granted you another day? Family household noises can quickly command your attention and call you to move to your daily morning routine. For some of us, our thoughts are flooded by the needs of the day before God even has a chance to get as much as a "Thank you, Lord, for another day."

Some begin the day with a complaint on their lips. As you embark on your strategy to have a deeper prayer life, will you waste your precious moments of connecting to God by complaining, or will you be filled with thanksgiving for the new opportunity of another day? Do a self-check. Do you start your day by focusing on what's wrong? Focusing on life's negatives first thing in the morning is no way to begin your day!

Complaining can be a contagious attitudinal lifestyle that blocks the joy and peace that God can bring into our lives. A cantankerous spirit has the capacity to kill joy and relationships.

If your day starts with everything that's wrong, you're probably spending more time complaining than you realize. Think about how many times a day you disparage your circumstances. Record how many words of thanksgiving flow from your lips within the same time frame.

An attitude of ingratitude blocks your ability to connect to God, because your focus is negative rather than positive. Instead of being critical and negative about things that are beyond your control, use them as an opportunity to strengthen your relationship to the Lord. Yes, it's tough, because complaining can become your comfort zone. Focus your thoughts on the blessings you have rather than the circumstances that are out of sorts. You're not dismissing reality; rather, you're speaking or praying a new reality. Speak those things as if they were, or pray that they have already happened (see Romans 4:17, Mark 11:24).

While the Apostle Paul was confined to a Roman prison, he wrote to the Philippian church: "Whatever is true, whatever is noble, whatever is right, whatever is pure, whatever is lovely, whatever is admirable—if anything is excellent or praiseworthy—think about such things" (Phil. 4:8 NIV). If an incarcerated Paul could encourage others to focus on life's positives, what's your excuse?

If you're comfortable being a complainer, you won't feel like devoting energy to moving out of your mode of grumbling about life. If you find it difficult to let go of complaining, employ the strategy of intentionality to ask God to change your attitude. Pray for a specified amount of time each day for God to fix your thoughts on the blessings and the positives in your life.

Use the principle of small, deliberate steps to help you let go of whining and embrace positive engagement with the Lord. Cut down your complaining time by 10 percent as you increase your positive prayer time connecting to God by 10 percent. That may be hard for you to measure, but make a conscious and concerted effort to focus more on positives and less on negatives. Commit to putting your daily gripes in the hands of God, and give God praise and thanksgiving for the many, many blessings you have but have probably forgotten.

Brother Brown prayed every Sunday at Bethel, Chesapeake City. His prayer echoed the prayers of our ancestors who prayed thanksgiving for eyes to see, hands to use, food to eat, and that their bed was not their cooling board or sheets their winding sheets for burial. Try this updated version:

Dear God, I thank you for another day. I'm grateful to be in my right mind, with the ability to raise my body out of bed and prepare for my day. I know many would desire to get out of bed, but they do not have the physical or mental capacity to do so. Thank you that I have a roof over my head. I am blessed to live in a land of great comfort. I thank you that I live in a nation of freedom, that I am able to pray at any point in my day.

Help me to examine my own attitude. Open my spiritual eyes to see how I may be contributing to my own unhappiness. Lord, I'm grateful.

Thank you for my family, dear God. We fuss at each other, but I thank you for the people in my life who love me enough to fuss. My life would not be the same without them.

Lord, I want to focus on the blessings of my life rather than complaining about the things I cannot change. Please strengthen my mind to stay fixed on your goodness rather than on what I think is missing. Thank you for a life that is full and rich and good. I commit to showing my gratitude for the blessings you give by helping others and showing them the love of Christ through my actions. I pray this in Jesus' name. Amen.

Loosen your grip on gripes so that your connection to God reveals the awesome power of the divine to radically change your life!

"Fix It, Father"

My father was an AAU (Association of American Universities) track star in the late 1930s at the University of Wisconsin. After graduation, among other things, he taught at Caver Vocational High School prior to beginning a career with the federal government. My father wanted at least one of his two children to follow in his track shoes. Since my brother played football, that left me. He tried me at the hundred-yard dash, but I was too slow. Undeterred, he tried me at the 880, but I had no endurance. Then he tried me at the pole vault, but I was afraid of heights. Determined to find the place where I fit, my father tried me at the long jump. I had no jump in me. He finally tried me at the high jump, where I showed some potential. He then turned me over to the assistant coach.

In order to cultivate my budding abilities at high jumping, I had to make some changes in my lifestyle. First, I had to practice every day. Then, I had to eat training table food, which meant no sugar, French fries, or hamburgers. I had to practice with the boys because there were very few high-jumping girls at the time. When it came time for me to practice, the assistant coach to whom I was assigned placed the bar higher for me than for my teammates.

Feeling somewhat persecuted, I went to my dad and asked him to fix it for me. He didn't, instead sending me back to the assistant coach. It happened again and again, and still my dad refused to fix the situation for me. Finally the community race day came. We took the field for our various events. The judges took the average height of our jumps and placed the bar. The bar was placed at the height that I was used to in practice. My teammates didn't make it. I won the gold medal and retired at the top of my game! I had been practicing with the bar set higher, so I was ready on the day that it really counted.

Although years later I understood that his inaction was for my benefit, I asked my father why he didn't come to my rescue: "Why didn't you fix it for me?" He replied, "Because your potential was greater than your problem, and your problem brought out your potential." Sometimes we may get frustrated in prayer because God is not fixing our circumstances as quickly as we'd like or in the manner that we want.

I was an extremely frustrated runner, because I didn't want to do it, and I knew my father had the power to change my circumstances. But he didn't, because he had something better in mind for me. Trust God and avoid the pit of frustration when God does not fix your situation the way that you planned. God may have something better in mind for you!

I was victorious on race day because I was connected to my father, who knew my abilities better than I knew them. Because of the father-daughter bond we shared, I was willing to submit to his plan to mold and shape me into what I could become. I didn't go my own way, because I was connected to my father and he was connected to me. Even though I didn't understand why he was doing what he was doing, I trusted him.

When we are connected to God, we submit to God's plan even when we don't understand it. We endure situations that don't make sense or that we don't want to be in, because we're connected to God. We trust that God may not fix things the way we want or as quickly as we want, but our connection to God builds our trust that God can fix whatever is going on in our lives.

When you intentionally develop a deeper connection to God, be prepared that God will not always handle your life circumstances the way you want or in the time frame that you want.

Keep Praying Through the Dry Seasons

Have you ever awakened in the morning and, as you move through your day, it seems that everything is working against you? The project at work needs a fresh idea and you're coming up empty. The household or personal budget needs to be reworked but your expenses still outweigh your income. The traffic is working against you; the line at your favorite coffee shop is unusually long; you're trying to move forward and it feels like you're swimming upstream. You're in the fast lane and the slowpokes are right in front of you...or you're trying to change lanes and people won't let you in.

Some of our dry seasons are the handiwork of the enemy. It's not paranoia. Jesus confirms that the Devourer gets in the way of our answered prayer. In Daniel 10, a messenger of the

Lord assures Daniel that his prayer was answered the moment that it was uttered. Opposing forces delayed the answer getting to Daniel by twenty-one days. The angel had to fight his way through to get to Daniel. We know an enemy actively works at eroding our connection to God.

At times your own inadvertent actions may be blocking answers to your prayers. Doubt and unbelief can cause your petitions to go unfulfilled. Jesus tells us to have faith and not doubt (see Matthew 21:21). By maintaining our faith in God's power to answer our requests, we can move mountains.

Another major hindrance to answered prayer is unforgiveness. In Mark 11:25, Jesus explains the importance of faith and forgiveness: "But when you are praying, first forgive anyone you are holding a grudge against, so that your Father in heaven will forgive your sins, too" (NLT).

Finally, we cannot mistreat those we are obligated to care for and still expect God to honor our petitions. Peter cautions husbands to treat their wives with compassion and respect, "so your prayers will not be hindered" (1 Pet. 3:7 NLT).

Dry wilderness seasons will show up in your prayer life every now and then. During these times you can lose your desire to pray because it feels like nothing is happening. Jesus gives us an insider's technique to having power in prayer. John 10:10 offers encouragement for the dusty spells in our prayer life. The enemy may show up to steal our joy during arid times of unanswered prayer, but we have the confident assurance that Jesus has come to give us abundant life.

In Matthew 16:19, Jesus tells his disciples, "I will give you the keys of the kingdom of heaven; whatever you bind on earth will be bound in heaven, and whatever you loose on earth will be loosed in heaven" (NIV).

Bind means "to forbid something," and *loose* means "to declare something permissible." God has declared that we have the power to bind in the name of Jesus:

> *I bind sickness and pain and loose health into my body in the name of Jesus.*
>
> *I bind lack and limitation from manifesting in my life and loose prosperity from the Creator, who possesses the cattle on one thousand hills.*
>
> *I bind faithlessness and fear in my heart and loose the power of the Holy Spirit to direct my life and order my steps.*

What do we do when we cannot get what we want or need? What do we do when we're ready to move on but are caught between a rock and a hard place?

When you are in the dry seasons, you may pray as the psalmists prayed: *"How long, O Lord, how long?"* What began as an anxious plea concludes quite differently as the psalmist realizes that God's steadfast love will never let him go. The poet begins Psalm 13 with a cry and ends with a song; I will sing the LORD's praise (v. 6 NIV).

If you have no words in the dry spells, pray the Scriptures (see Psalm 62):

> *My soul only waits for the Lord. In silence I sit in anticipation for the one who is my rock and my salvation. Draw me out of the chaos of this world and into the calm of your*

intimacy. I breathe out chaos and breathe in calm; breathe out the chaotic experiences of living in an uncertain world and breathe in the calm of a peace that surpasses all understanding; breathe out chaotic personalities and breathe in the calm of a changeless Christ; breathe out ignorance and breathe in the calm of your wisdom that instructs me; breathe out my will and breathe in thy will be done.

When you are deeply connected to God through a consistent prayer life, you can start with a cry of lament and end up with a song. You may start out anxious or troubled and end up shouting praises. Hold on to your hope in the dry seasons. Stay connected. It's coming!

STEPPING-STONES

1. Identify space and time to pray.

2. Focus thoughts on a weekly Bible verse. Start with the book of Psalms or the Gospel of John.

3. Keep it simple—Sincere Sacred Supplication—just have a little talk with Jesus!

4. Use the 4S Method (Solitude, Submission, Service, and *Selah*) to direct your prayer connection to God.

5. Listen. Prayer is also a two-way street. Discern what God is revealing to you in prayer.

6. Be still in the presence of God (see Psalm 46:10).

7. Go to your local house of worship and pray at the altar or in the pew. This can be before and/or after worship, Bible study, meetings, or rehearsals.

8. Write your reflections and revelations in a book or journal.

9. Keep track of your prayer requests and answers in the same book or journal.

10. When God answers your prayer, tell the testimony as an encouragement for someone who is still waiting on his or her answer.

Discover

Do not merely listen to the word, and so deceive yourselves. Do what it says.

JAMES 1:22 NIV

You Christians look after a document containing enough dynamite to blow all civilisation to pieces, turn the world upside down, and bring peace to a battle-torn planet. But you treat it as though it is nothing more than a piece of literature.

—MAHATMA GANDHI

Karen Hartley spent Christmas Eve, 1997, trapped in an avalanche at a ski resort in Weber County, Utah, engulfed in the darkness and hovering between life and death. She had ventured out of bounds while on a ski trip when the accident occurred. A darkness descended upon her like what the ancients describe as the "dark night of the soul." It is what author Adele

Green, in her book *Can You See Me Naked? Grow in a Conscious Relationship*, describes as the place where you learn who you are, without people telling you.

Hartley was alone in the dark. Instead of giving up or curling into a fetal position to wait for death, she heard a song come to mind. She chose to dance to the tune in her head in the darkness of night. The next day she was rescued.

When Paul and Silas were locked up in a Roman jail, they could have given up. Instead, in the darkness of midnight, they prayed. And while they were singing, praying, and maybe even dancing in the dark, the jail doors suddenly flew open and they were free. In the gloom of night they received their liberation, and the jailer found salvation for himself and his family.

Hartley sang what came into her head and danced in the dark until help arrived. Paul and Silas prayed and sang in the dark until they were free.

Hartley retrieved her lyrics from past experiences. The songs that rose up within Paul and Silas at their darkest hour were the melodies of past experiences with God, which were tapped out like a sweet, sweet sound in their ears.

In the darkness of our challenges, God's Word is a lamp for our feet (see Psalm 119:105). As that Word unfolds in our lives, it gives us light and understanding (see Psalm 119:130). Scripture is not a flickering flame of mystics; we also have the Word made flesh who dwelt among us: His name is Jesus (see John 1:14). Discover God's Word and discover God.

Study the Bible

What do you study? Do you follow local, national, and international media? Do you pick up snippets of information from Twitter or other forms of social media? If someone else had the capacity to eavesdrop on your thoughts, would they be able to tell what you study? In other words, would the person listening think you are more influenced by Jesus than you are by Facebook or CNN, Fox or NPR?

When you see a trending issue on social media, you may decide to click on the link and find out more. Maybe your favorite celebrity couple split up, or a beloved entertainer died, or a natural disaster occurred. You want to know more.

Every day, God is leaving hashtagged messages all around you in an effort to pique your interest so that you will want to know more. Does God ever get your attention this way? A stranger engages you in a conversation about relationships, and you get curious (#songofsolomon). You read a story about someone who murdered a family member (#cainandabel). Maybe you get into an interesting conversation with a neighbor about the fact that God has a purpose for everyone (#Jeremiah29:11).

The Bible is a fascinating work because it never gets old or stale. Its stories are always alive and relevant. Its truths are timeless and enlightening.

What Makes the Bible Special?

If you enjoy eating watermelon in the summer, you know that when you cut a slice and prepare to eat it, there may be dozens of little dark seeds inside. Within those seeds is the potential to bear more fruit. Each piece of fruit has the power within it to reproduce itself. From the seeds in your apple comes the power to grow more apples. And from those apples, even more apples, and perhaps from those apples, an entire apple grove.

The Word of God is a lot like those fruit seeds. The Word has the power to reproduce itself. God's promises in the Bible are reproduced in my life. Inside God's Word is the seed to reproduce peace, power, and wisdom. Within God's Word are stories with wisdom to give you guidance and direction and prophecies to give you hope and promises to give you assurance.

Some of those stories are shocking, with as much drama as a reality television show. Sarah and Hagar had their own drama going, and so did Hannah and Peninnah, but they are not the Real Housewives of Ephraim. Their lifestyles are not fabricated and overglamorized to gain ratings. Their stories are recorded for our edification and enlightenment.

During the 2015 Hampton Ministers' Conference, I heard Dr. John Kinney, senior vice president of Virginia Union University, offer an intriguing analogy about the Word of God. He shared a story about a unique modification of watermelons. During the 1980s, a Japanese farmer started growing watermelons in square containers. As they grew, they took on the shape of the vessel that enclosed them. The square watermelons were easier to store in compact spaces. On the outside, it would seem that this unknown farmer had changed the nature of watermelons. But any horticulturist would tell you that even though the melons had been forced into a square shape, if one planted the seeds of the square watermelon, the new ones would grow in their original rounded shape. So it is with Scripture. There are many different translations and paraphrases of the Bible, and most of us have our favorite. Even though the words may be contemporized for the limited spaces of human understanding, the essence and origin of God's Word is unchanged.

A Book of Discovery

The Bible is divine truth, but the Word is also a wonderful repository of human experiences. There's nothing going on today that is really new in terms of human nature or behavior. Since the creation of Adam and Eve, people have experienced every kind of predicament imaginable.

- Lying—Abraham claimed his wife, Sarah, was his sister because he was afraid (see Genesis 20).

- Murder—Cain murdered his brother, Abel (see Genesis 4).

- Theft—Jacob stole his brother Esau's birthright via deception (see Genesis 27).

- Sibling rivalry—Joseph's brothers were jealous of his relationship with their father, Jacob (see Genesis 37).

- Adultery—David engaged in an adulterous relationship with Bathsheba (see 2 Samuel 11).

- Cohabitation—The Samaritan woman at the well was living with a man who was not her husband (see John 4).

- Anger—Peter was a hothead who once cut off a Roman servant's ear out of anger (see John 18).

- Pregnancy out of wedlock—Mary, the mother of Jesus, became pregnant as an unwed teenager (see Luke 1).

- Unrequited love—Peninnah had many babies for Elkanah, but he did not have the love for her that he had for Hannah (see 1 Samuel 1).

- Search for meaning and purpose—Gideon wasn't sure that God was calling him and needed signs (see Judges 6).

- Disobedience to God—Jonah refused to go to Nineveh to evangelize because he despised the people (see Jonah 1).

- Questioning God—The prophet Habakkuk questioned God's inaction in the midst of troubling times (see Habakkuk 1).

- Suffering—Job was a righteous man but still lost everything that mattered (see Job 1).

- Depression—Elijah successfully defeated the prophets of Baal but still ran away from Jezebel and ended up hiding in a cave (see 1 Kings 19).

- Sudden turnarounds—Paul was in a Roman jail (see Philippians 1:1–26).

- Incest—Amnon obsessed after his sister (see 2 Samuel 13).

God's Word reveals that the issues with which human beings grapple have not changed. Children still think their parents don't understand what's happening in the modern world, like the prodigal son who left home to explore life elsewhere. As we read about the struggles of other human beings, and discover that God still loved them and desired to stay in relationship with them, we gain affirmation of our value in God's sight.

We can be both comforted and encouraged to find personalities in the Bible who have trod paths similar to ours. As you read Bible stories about people and their experiences, you see yourself reflected in their experiences. Reading about Moses at the burning bush, you see your own insecurities and doubts. But as you continue reading the story of Moses' ascension as the great but fallible leader who brought Israel out of bondage in Egypt, you see in yourself one who can accomplish great things, guided by the hand of God. You empathize with Hannah, a faithful servant of God wanting something so badly that she prayed mightily, without regard to how undignified she looked while doing so. Reading the Psalms can help you connect with David's anxieties, frustrations, failings, and laments as he strived to live in a manner pleasing to God. Finding such kindred spirits also affirms for us that God's power to handle any circumstance has not diminished.

In fourteen years of Circle encounters in two congregations, only a handful of women never shared. On one particular night, a Circle sister started to cry uncontrollably. The other women rushed to console her. Her voice railed until it became raspy. We prayed and cried, prayed and cried, until she got to the place where she could let go with a sigh.

A few days later in private she shared with me what had happened to her that night in the Circle. For years she had blamed herself for the physical challenges of her son. She had been very cavalier about her pregnancy and didn't take care of herself as directed by her physician. She smoked, drank alcohol excessively, and did drugs.

After her son was born, his development was slow both physically and mentally. She beat herself up about his condition on a daily basis. It was all she could do just to get through the day as his caregiver.

In the Circle, we explored the Bible verses concerning Mephibosheth (see 2 Samuel 9). His caregiver dropped him in the midst of a crisis; the boy was lame in both feet and unable to take care of himself. Yet, he found favor in the sight of King David, who saw to his provision.

My Circle member realized that night that both she and her son had found favor in the Lord in spite of her reckless actions. She had found the right doctor, the right counselor, the right school, the right scholarship, and the right medications that provided for her son beyond what she could do.

She saw her life reflected in the story of Mephibosheth. Hers were tears of joy, not sadness. She screamed at the realization how God had blessed her in spite of herself.

Do You Speak Bible?

Our nation is becoming increasingly diverse, and it is possible to be in an environment where no one is speaking a language we understand. Maybe you've experienced this if you've traveled to a non-English-speaking country. But what if the people are speaking English, and you still can't understand what they're talking about? Do you feel that way when people start talking about the Bible? Are they speaking a language you don't understand?

People who regularly study God's Word generally have a ready mental reference log of Scriptures and circumstances to affirm or provide insight regarding their current condition. If you hear someone say that God always provides a ram in the bush, do you understand that it means God will make a way when there seems to be no other way? In Genesis 22:1–14, God provided a way for faithful Abraham out of a seemingly impossible situation.

Dozens of colloquialisms in our language are rooted in the Bible, but if you've never read it, the fullness of their meaning may elude you. While you may understand the context in which a phrase is used, the deeper meaning never gains full expression. So when other people are speaking about biblical things, or even when the preacher is delivering a sermon, how can you understand what it means if you don't speak Bible? It's like listening to someone speak a foreign language. You may understand a word here and there; you may understand the gist of the message. But you miss major portions of what's being conveyed because you don't speak the language. Some people stop going to church because they don't speak the language. They have no idea what the preacher is talking about, although everybody else seems to get it.

Whether you've been studying the Bible for years or whether you recognize only a few familiar passages, there's always something new to discover—new understandings of familiar stories, new truths previously overlooked, new insights garnered from spiritual maturity.

The study of God's Word should engage both the mind and the heart, as we are to love the Lord with all our heart and mind. My mind is renewed by God's Word. God's Word transforms my heart. It changes what I think in my mind. God's Word changes how I live out of my heart.

Psalm 23; John 3:16; and the Lord's Prayer were the first Bible verses I memorized as a child. We'd recite the Twenty-Third Psalm in Sunday school or for special services in church. When someone gave their life to Jesus Christ, the whole church would recite John 3:16. Our very first lessons in evangelism taught us to share that God loved us so much that God gave us Jesus, God's only Son. And if we believe this, we will not perish but will have eternal life. Although I could recite it, it wasn't until I believed it that my life changed dramatically. The Word in my head finally reached my heart.

Failure to read the Word of God is a failure to utilize available power. Likewise, reading your Bible without availing yourself of its power is like buying a million-dollar race car to drive to the grocery store once a week. Know the authority of God's Word and engage its power in your life. Give yourself more power by taking a small step and commit to more time for greater reflection in God's Word.

A Plan for Discovery

You wake up one morning and decide you want to check climbing Mount Kilimanjaro off your bucket list. You can't just pack a bag and hop on a flight to Tanzania, because you don't haphazardly venture into unknown territory. To gain the most out of your trip, a number of preparations are needed. You need some preliminary information to know what to expect, how to pack, how much it will cost, and how long the trip will last.

That's what it means to engage in personal Bible study. Some things need to be in place before you begin. First, establish an adequate amount of time for study and reflection. Whether you decide to spend fifteen minutes, thirty minutes, or an hour in

Bible study, an established time frame will help you determine how to proceed. If you'll do better with a study partner, invite your spouse or a friend who also wants to learn more about the Bible to join you. Once you have established time parameters, develop a consistent plan for studying God's Word.

Technology has revolutionized our ability to gain information and makes discovery of God's Word easier. You can read the Bible using a traditional bound volume or via the Internet. Read the Bible on your phone, your tablet, or your computer. Listen to the Bible in audio format in your car or when you go to sleep. Scripture is available online in virtually every translation or paraphrase and in many different languages. Learn the Word on the commute to and from your place of employment, or on a road or shopping trip. The Bible on audiotape is great listening during the ride. You can read the Bible on your mobile phone as you wait in line to get your driver's license renewed. Hundreds if not thousands of free or affordable Bible study plans from reputable teachers and institutions are also available to guide your learning path. Join an e-mail Bible study group with disciples around the world. There are resources to read the entire Bible in thirty, sixty, or ninety days as well as to read the Bible incrementally in one year.

If you choose to begin reading without a specific plan, start with the Gospel of John and keep reading until the Holy Spirit tells you to stop. John's Gospel reveals to us the person of Jesus Christ—who he is, why he came, and how he ministered while on earth. From John's account, a good transition would be the Acts of the Apostles. From Acts, venture through the remainder of the Epistles in the New Testament and on to Revelation. Then you will be ready to go to the beginning of the Bible and read the book of Genesis and continue through the Old Testament into the remaining three Gospels of the New Testament.

Once you have established a time and a plan, pray for understanding before you study. Ask God to grant you inspiration, revelation, knowledge, and understanding as you study. Pray for focus so that you will push aside details of the world to gain understanding. Your petition should be that the Holy Spirit empowers you to sit and concentrate on the Word and how it applies to your life. Reading a devotional piece may also be a good opener for personal Bible study to give you a point of focus and reflection before study. As you prepare to study, invite the Holy Spirit to empower your understanding, because gaining biblical knowledge is not simply a matter of intelligence.

If you have a hard time understanding a more traditional translation, or are distracted by *thee, thou, beget,* and *begat,* consider a contemporary English Bible translation. You may even find a Bible paraphrase helpful. Some readers gain greater understanding reading a paraphrase version, which restates the words of the original biblical languages using contemporary words and sentence structures. Some readers prefer to read a Bible translation, which converts the original Hebrew, Greek, and Aramaic words of the Bible into English or another language.

Now you're in the Word! As you read, an important study tool is to remember not to interpret the Word of God in isolation. That means you don't read one verse or passage of Scripture and determine, "That's it! The Bible says right here we're supposed to..." Take your investigation a bit further. Read before and after the passage to gain a broader understanding. Consult a Bible dictionary or commentary for clarification and context. Then study Bible resources to find out if there is another Scripture that supports or validates the truth of that passage. Did Jesus address the matter, either directly or indirectly? Look for confirmation in the text.

Reading the Bible Helps You Mature Spiritually

As you learn Scripture, make declarations of God's Word over your life. Release the power of God's Word in your life. Pray the Scriptures like David did: "To You, O LORD, I lift up my soul. O my God, I trust in You; let me not be ashamed; let not my enemies triumph over me" (Ps. 25:1–2 NKJV). Or like Hannah did: "My heart rejoices in the LORD; my horn is exalted in the LORD...No one is holy like the LORD, for there is none besides You, nor is there any rock like our God" (1 Sam. 2:1–2 NKJV).

And as you learn the power in God's Word, God's Spirit gets involved. The learning going on in your head travels to your heart. Then, when moments of truth come long after the

Bible study session, you will examine yourself and ask questions like "Am I going to tell the truth, or will I lie?" What does the Word tell you to do?

As you read and gain understanding, God's Word teaches you a standard of how to live that is directly juxtaposed to what the world says. The world says, "Don't let anyone get anything over on you." Jesus says, "Love your enemies; love those who try to use you."

Only through studying God's Word can we begin to absorb the high calling of our faith. Being a Christian is tough. It's hard to forgive the people who repeatedly hurt you, as Jesus commands in Matthew 18:22. It's hard to remain faithful to God's commandments when other people seem to do anything they want and still prosper, as Psalm 73 details.

There's an interesting photo on the Internet of an ordinary house cat walking past no less than a dozen German shepherds who are seated at attention. No matter how badly the dogs may want to break loose and chase the cat with gusto, they remain in position. Those dogs did not assume and maintain their posture by accident. They resisted the temptation to do what comes naturally to them because of their obedience to the training they had been given.

That visual reminds us that as disciples seeking to live God's Word, there are some things we should be disciplined enough to let pass us by. Not every opportunity should be pursued simply because it crosses our path. Not every relationship should be pursued simply because the opportunity passes our way. We ought to let some things pass by because we are disciplined through the practice of obedience to God's Word.

Obedience is a sign of true discipleship and of a right relationship with Christ. Conformity to Jesus' teachings is how the Twelve showed that they loved Christ. In John 14:15, Jesus says to his disciples, "If you love me, obey my commandments" (NLT).

Don't just study the Bible; declare the Word out loud, release it into the atmosphere. Then keep declaring God's Word until what is spoken in the Spirit manifests itself in the natural world. Sure, it sounds too strange to be true, but God's Word is true and it can work for you.

Feed Yourself

When our children were young, the act of feeding them was a special bonding experience. As I fed them each small spoonfuls of baby food, they eagerly consumed what was provided for them. Every now and then a certain jar of food would not appeal to them. Sometimes they would want to play rather than eat. But eventually they all grew and learned how to feed themselves. Even when my husband and I were still providing the food, they learned how to feed themselves without depending on us.

Now that our children are grown, one with a child of their own, imagine how difficult life would be for them if they had never learned to feed themselves. Instead of looking for some-one to feed them, our children are now feeding themselves and others.

There comes a time in all our lives when we have to learn to feed ourselves—physically and spiritually. None of us can go through our spiritual life expecting others to feed us the Word until we are satisfied. Every disciple is invited to journey from the milk of the Word to the meat of the Word. That takes place through consistent study of God's Word, both at home and in a small-group setting. A Sunday morning sermon won't give it to you completely. Your favorite televangelist can't give you all the teaching you need.

There comes a time when you need to find inspiration for yourself. Your experience becomes the catalyst through which God's Word is made alive and you come to greater under-standing. John 3:16 is simply rote until you realize that God so loved (insert your name here) that God gave God's Son so that (insert your name here), who believes in him, would have everlasting life. When you recognize that the "whosoever" in that passage is you, that's a powerful moment!

God's promise in Jeremiah 29:11 is feel-good words, until you recognize that God has pulled you out of what might have been a disastrous situation and directed you to a place that benefits you tremendously.

Proverbs 16:3 seems like good words to live by, until you realize that God has blessed you with opportunity that you could never have orchestrated yourself.

Job 1:21 is lofty words of faith, until you lose something you treasure deeply, but deep within you know everything will be all right because everything in your life is, and always has been, in God's hands.

I learned Psalm 23 by rote as a child attending Sunday school and church services. But the full impact of David's psalm did not hit home for me until I was living in Africa during my first tenure as bishop of the Eighteenth Episcopal District of the AME Church, which encompasses southeast Africa. My family and friends were back in the States. I was far away from the support system I had known all my life and was traveling with local AMEs to various churches in my district. Sometimes they would say things like "Bishop, we can't stay long at this church. We have to get back across the border before it gets dark." That was when I got the full understanding of how God's goodness and mercy follow me. I don't want goodness and mercy to have to put a GPS on me!

The experiences that happen to us can bring God's Word before us face-first. *BAM!* Sometimes there are divine moments when God steps in, and everything after that moment is absolutely different. You see things differently because you are not the same. You treat situations differently in God's divine moments because everything after that changes. That's what happens after salvation. You can't treat the Bible like it's just an interesting book. You can't just treat it as a history book or an anthropological study. The Word of God is living and has the power to mold and shape us into disciples who strive to achieve the high calling.

STEPPING-STONES

1. Identify a regular place and time to read the Bible. Pray before you study, whether privately or corporately.

2. Start small and increase your amount of reading in manageable increments.

3. Reflect on how God has blessed you in spite of yourself.

4. Focus your thoughts on 2 Timothy 2:15 and reflect on the purpose and power of Scripture.

5. Use a weekly, a monthly, or an annual Bible reading plan. Plans are available online or in book form at Christian bookstores.

6. Choose a focal verse from your study and write it on a note card. Put it in a place where you can see it throughout the day or evening. Speak it aloud when you have the opportunity.

7. Enter the focal Bible verse into your digital devices so you can pull it up to read often.

8. If you do not have a Bible reading plan, begin with the Gospel of John, then read the Epistles before going

to Genesis. Then keep reading until you have read all sixty-six books. Try a few verses or a chapter a day until you have completely read the Bible.

9. Use a contemporary translation or paraphrase to read Bible stories to your children and grandchildren as bedtime stories.

10. Identify the promises of God as you read. Commit them to memory or record them on your mobile phone or tablet.

11. Use a Bible you can understand clearly, and don't limit yourself to one version.

12. Be patient with yourself, and recognize that studying God's Word is a lifelong pursuit.

13. Look for audiovisual aids online to supplement your learning experience.

Celebrate

*Let's see how inventive we can be in encouraging love
and helping out, not avoiding worshiping together as
some do but spurring each other on, especially as we
see the big Day approaching.*

HEBREWS 10:24–25 MSG

*As worship begins in holy expectancy, it ends in
holy obedience...Holy obedience saves worship from
becoming an opiate, an escape from the pressing needs
of modern life.*

RICHARD FOSTER

Sometimes, the only thing that can feed your soul is worship.

Candidating for the episcopacy in the African Methodist
Church tradition is exhausting. There are weeks of traveling to
other episcopal districts in North America and beyond. Count-
less hours are spent in dialogue with clergy and lay leadership

while creating a campaign strategy to help you stand out in a crowded field. Speeches are made in conference settings, on the sidewalks, in elevators, in hotel lobbies, or anywhere there is a listening ear. Most of the time, campaign encounters are positive. Sometimes, however, they are not.

After one particularly grueling campaign trip, I was rushing back to Baltimore for Sunday services at Payne Memorial. As our family car turned the corner from Druid Hill Avenue onto Laurens Street, the hunger pains for worship within me grew intense. All I could see was the glow of the lights through the massive stained glass windows high above the choir stand behind the pulpit. It was an awesome sight.

I was moved to tears in anticipation of being in glorious Holy Spirit–led worship. I started singing, "Bread of heaven, feed me until I want no more, feed me until I want no more" (from the hymn "Guide Me, O Thou Great Jehovah," *AMEC Hymnal*). My family, three children and one husband, were all looking at me with amazement. The melodious song I was singing in my heart came out of my mouth very off-key! I'm glad God listens to the heart!

The hunger pains for worship can happen when you are overwhelmed with gratitude over God's blessings. Maybe nothing in particular has happened; you just realize that you're tremendously blessed. Everyone in your household is well. Your job is work that you enjoy and it pays you well. You've received blessings you didn't work for and could never earn. You have more blessings than you could ever have imagined, and every fiber of your being calls out to express your gratitude.

Our need for purgative expressions of praise and thanksgiving do not contain themselves to Sunday morning. Fortunately, we never have to make an appointment to celebrate and engage with the Creator of the universe.

In the African American church context, from the time of the "invisible" slave church, worship has been as much catharsis as celebration—a release of both joy and sorrow, an expression of lament over things that have happened and joy for the faith that beacons that bright side somewhere. We have shouted out our hurts. We've shouted our praises of thanksgiving. We've sat quietly in reflective awe of almighty God. We let go of the concerns of this world to reach for the things of God. We move from our own agenda to God's.

Sometimes when you are far away from a house of worship, you have a hunger for the preached Word of God and desire to glorify the Lord with the sounds of praise through worship.

In times of tension—among the nations, among families, amid opposing people groups—basking in the presence of God is a welcome respite. When we come before God in our humanity and humility, we find reprieve from the world's craziness, contempt, and confusion. Worship is the place where life is no longer a blur. In the flow of worship, we recognize that our lives depend on God alone—not on finances, on family, or on friends. As we dwell in this sacred place, we learn that our future is secure, so we can live abundantly. In God's presence, we are energized and filled with love, joy, and peace.

We have an open invitation to enter the presence of God, and we can enter through a number of open doors in the context of worship. Giving adoration to God is a personal expression, and authentic worship is as personal and unique as the individual. We may enter through prayer. We may enter through meditation. We also may enter through the celebration of God's movement in our lives. As we live in the light of God's presence, we will shine brightly. "Let your light so shine..."

Choose Your Place to Celebrate

Everybody ought to have a place of celebration—where they can, as Jesus did, worship God in spirit and in truth (see John 4:24). The Bible is replete with examples of faithful people who were blessed by their willingness to seek the face of God through worship.

In the Old Testament, before there were synagogues or temples, it was not uncommon for the faithful to build an altar to worship the Lord.

- Noah built an altar to the Lord because God remembered him and all the animals in the ark and allowed them to survive the flood (see Genesis 8:20).

- Abraham built an altar after God promised to give his descendants the land inhabited by the Canaanites (see Genesis 12:5–7).

- After Abraham traveled farther to Bethel, he built an altar and worshipped God there. He again worshipped there after his sojourn to Egypt (see Genesis 12–13).

Through his worship encounters, Abraham grew closer to God.

- Following the example of his father, Isaac built an altar and worshipped God after God affirmed the promise made to his father (see Genesis 26:25).

- The Israelites built an altar to the Lord after they crossed the Jordan River to the Promised Land (see Deuteronomy 27:4–7).

Many others built altars, but Abraham set the example to begin a family tradition of building altars to worship God. His son, Isaac, built an altar to worship God. So did his grandson, Jacob. When your children see that you do not reserve praise and worship for the church sanctuary, it will set a foundation for them to freely offer praise and worship to God.

Our Children Are Watching

It is important that parents pass on faith to their progeny by example—and children can remember only what they have gotten. When your children are grown and facing difficult situations like young Pastor Timothy did (see 1 Timothy 4), fads, fashion, trends, ToryBurch, and Michael Kors can't help. But if you have passed on to your children a legacy of faith, they will be able to make it through the difficult times.

Human beings remember what they see and experience

more than what they are told. Your children may not praise God away from a church building unless that behavior has been modeled at home.

Timothy's mother began teaching him when he was an infant. She didn't wait until he was a troubled teenager. You can't afford to wait until the world has conditioned your children to be everything but faithful and then tell them, "Oh, by the way, before you leave from home, I need to tell you what faith can do."

Habits of praise have to be instilled when children are young. Children need to hear their parents say, "Praise the Lord!" They need to see them worship. Parents need to teach their children, by precept and example, how they can survive the heat of troubling times. When your children know that God will make a way, they won't run to the dope man or a liquor bottle to drown their sorrows. They will exercise their faith.

Isaac saw his father build an altar at Mount Moriah. What better tribute to good parenting than to hear an adult say, "I remember Momma doing her praise dance when God came through for her unexpectedly." Or they can recall how their father was not ashamed to stop and say, "Praise the Lord! Glory to God! Thank you, Jesus!"

Jeremiah Wright, pastor emeritus of Trinity United Church of Christ in Chicago, in his sermon "The Audacity of Hope" (*What Makes You So Strong?* Judson Press, 1993, p. 97), tells the story of his parents praising God in the aftermath of his arrest for larceny auto theft. Wright was fifteen at the time, sitting alone in his bedroom, contrite, after his parents posted his bond. He could hear them in the next room, praying and saying, "Thank you, Lord. Thank you, Lord." At the time, he could not understand what they could possibly be thanking God for. As he grew in faith, however, he understood they were praising God in faith for what their son would become, not for what he was at that moment.

God gives the responsibility of teaching faith to parents, not the church. Model faith for your children and for future generations. Give God praise as you tell others of the victories that God has brought you through.

Check Your Baggage at the Door

The unnamed woman labeled a sinner in Luke 7:36–50 teaches us a valuable lesson on worship. She didn't wait for a formal worship opportunity to show honor to Jesus. She also didn't let her designation as a sinner prevent her from giving him due praise. This woman's desire was to worship Jesus, and she wasn't going to let anyone stop her.

The uninvited woman came to Simon's house seeking Jesus. She probably had heard how he had forgiven the sins of many and that they had been healed of their infirmities. This woman didn't have a physical infirmity. Nevertheless, she had a less than sterling reputation. She wanted to be forgiven and restored.

There were throngs of people outside the Pharisee's house, but this woman had made up her mind to get to Jesus. She didn't let her personal baggage hold her back from finding

Jesus. She cast aside cultural imperatives, past behavior, and public opinion as she made her way to him.

Baggage can hinder us from true worship. What baggage? Anything that steals your attention from God and hinders your worship is baggage. Often people carry attitudes and issues that hinder them from worship, even while they're sitting in church. If you desire to worship God and let God take you higher, check your baggage at the door of your spirit and give God full rein. It doesn't matter whether you worship in church or at home.

This woman's example of courage can help us all break out of a worship comfort zone and learn some lessons. First, we should let nothing hinder us from worship. Second, no price is too great for the privilege of giving praise. Third, Jesus honors our sincere desire to worship him.

This woman wanted to give, but many believers think only of what they can receive from a worship encounter with God. Hebrews 13:15 tells us to offer a sacrifice of praise. That means we offer our worship even if we're not feeling worshipful at the outset.

Praise Your Way Through It

Wouldn't it be great if life was rosy all the time and all we felt like doing was walking around saying "Praise the Lord" to everybody we meet? But that's not real life. When life turns downward, we cannot give in and give up. That's when it's most important to give praise to God.

The prophet Habakkuk had been wrestling with a perplexing problem. It just didn't seem fair that the wicked prospered while God's people were in despair. But his perspective changed along the way, and he began to praise God instead of complain.

In Habakkuk 3, the prophet saturated his mind with the greatness of God. Prior to this, all he talked about was the problems God's people were having with the Babylonians. But once he gained assurance that God was in control despite the circumstances, Habakkuk was through worrying about the problems.

Habakkuk gives us great insight about praising our way through our problems. The prophet takes his eyes off his circumstances and focuses on God. The life challenges we face are never about the Babylonians in our lives. It's always about God.

True worship means offering oneself to God. It is giving God praise because of and in spite of our circumstances. Habakkuk determined that despite all he was going through and might have yet to go through, he would rejoice in the Lord. Praising God through everything is based not on *how* you praise, but rather *when* you praise. Praise God in all things, under all conditions, in all circumstances.

Habakkuk closed his prophecy in chapter 3 with an uncertain future, but he never stopped praising God. Through praise, Habakkuk found the strength to climb his mountain of despair.

Paul and Silas also faced an uncertain future, but that did not prevent them from praising and worshipping God as they sat in a dark, dank prison cell at midnight. Thelonius Monk wrote a jazz song about midnight that was full of dread and despair. But Wilson Pickett sang an R & B song about the midnight hour that he eagerly anticipated. Our song in the midnight hour should be one of praise, not defeat or sorrow. We who hope in the Lord can sing praises even in the darkest hour because of his promises.

Sometimes all you can sing is "It Is Well with My Soul." Writer Horatio Spafford was a successful lawyer who grieved after his two-year-old son and his four daughters perished during an ocean voyage accident. He had suffered huge financial losses during the 1871 Great Chicago Fire and had sent his family to Europe on the SS *Ville du Havre*. He had to stay behind to handle business affairs. His wife sent him the grave news: "Saved alone."

As Spafford journeyed to join his wife he wrote:

When peace, like a river, attendeth my way,
When sorrows like sea billows roll;
Whatever my lot, Thou hast taught me to know [or *say*]
It is well, it is well, with my soul.

Every person has had some midnights. We have had to sing in faith before we saw the manifestation of that for which we hoped.

You probably can look back over some distressing circumstances in your life and recognize that God was right there—at your bedside, in your car seat, in your work cubicle, in your kitchen, in your bathroom—wherever a flood of trouble seemed about to overtake you. As you continue to worship and praise

God, the Lord's track record in your life tells you that you can trust and depend on God in the midnight hours of your life.

Be Good for Nothing

Satan asked God: "Is Job good for nothing?" That's an intriguing question that could be asked of every child of God. Ask yourself, "Do I worship God, serve God, and love God only for what I can get out of it?"

Job was a well-to-do businessman with a family he loved. He loved God even more and worshipped God faithfully. Job was without moral failure. He even made offerings on behalf of his children, just in case they did something wrong that he didn't know about.

He was so faithful that God even bragged on him to Satan, "Have you considered my servant Job?"

Satan responds by saying, "Of course Job worships you. Look at what you've done for him!" And it was true. Job 1:3 describes Job as the greatest man of all the people in the East. Then Satan offers: "If you really want to see what Job is made of, allow the winds of adversity to blow against his life, and then let's see how high he jumps in church on Sunday."

Satan accused Job of having quid pro quo faith, or tit for tat: Job was good because of the benefits he received. We worship God not just for what we receive; we worship God for who God is! Our pursuit of the blessings should never outweigh our pursuit of the Blesser.

Transaction or Transformation?

There's a difference between transactional worship and transformational worship. Transactional worship relates to God only as one who blesses and gives to us. This kind of approach ignores the values and standards that disciples are expected to uphold. Transactional worship is all about getting from God. It's about getting tangible items to enhance our lifestyle rather than a changed heart.

By contrast, transformational worship means giving to God. When we are praising God and making worship a priority, our service comes forth. In giving our heart to God we are transformed, and we can envision and seek God's purpose for our lives, because our minds are connected into God's agenda.

Transactional worship is a theology that holds God to promises that God never made. God never promised that if we sing in the choir we won't lose our job. God never promised that if we shout louder than anybody else, we'll never have money trouble. God never promised that if we come to church every Sunday we won't get sick.

Worship is not a transaction with God. There's nothing we can give God, because God already owns it all. So what can we possibly think God needs from us?

At the lowest point in his life, Job still worshipped God. With no home, no children, no health, and no resources, he said, "The LORD gave, and the LORD has taken away; blessed be the name of the LORD" (Job 1:21 ESV). The pursuit of the blessings should never outweigh the pursuit of the Blesser. True worship pursues the Blesser.

What's Your Style?

Most of us are aware that we have a personal style. It influences the clothes we wear, the car we drive, and how we decorate our home. We each have a style of worship, too. The Bible does not give us a mandated protocol for worship, except that we do so in spirit and in truth (see John 4:24).

We each respond differently to the presence of Christ. Mary wanted to sit at Jesus' feet listening to the Word teach the Word. She was undeterred by the preparation activity around her (see Luke 10). Meanwhile, Martha wanted to organize the environment for the unexpected visit, thus serving Christ differently. We need both Marys and Marthas in church—the worshipper and the worker, the praiser and the preparer—because each sister's style of response had its own value.

Some people will stand and shout in praise. Others may simply shed a tear. Some people feel the Word in nondemonstrative ways and may revere God through their silence. Still others are believers who just have to give a vocal response to God's presence—singing or shouting or praising. They make a joyful noise and cannot simply sit in silence. Then there are people who respond physically—they dance, they run around the sanctuary, they high-five someone nearby, or they slap the back of the pew.

All of these forms of worship can be authentic worship. No one can invalidate someone else's style of responding to the presence of the Lord. God reaches people and speaks to them differently. Elijah heard God speaking in a still, small voice in the mountain (see 1 Kings 19:11–13) and Job heard God from a whirlwind (see Job 38:1). Yet, the voice of God spoke at Jesus' baptism as an audible voice, but sounded to Ezekiel as many roaring waters (see Ezekiel 43:2).

God speaks in ways that disciples can hear, and those listening respond in personal ways. Find the worship center where you believe God is speaking to you. If you have not joined a church already, you may have to visit a few before you find one that fits. You may find a church that's different from the one you grew up in; nevertheless, it fits. If you visit a church that's not your style, it's not an indictment against you or the worshippers in that church. It's just different.

Go to any coffeehouse and they will have many different coffee strengths and creamer flavors. None of them are wrong or right. They're just different. The place where you worship may be different from every other church you've ever been to, but if it is Bible centered, Christ focused, and Holy Spirit led, you will experience a close encounter of the God kind.

"Hello" from God

Occasionally, we experience divine moments when we encounter the presence of God, and nothing is the same afterward. Authentic worship is where we open ourselves totally to God and hold nothing back! It's like getting a personal "Hello" from God.

It happened to Isaiah. The prophet reveals: "In the year that King Uzziah died, I saw the Lord, high and exalted, seated on a throne; and the train of his robe filled the temple" (Isa. 6:1 NIV). He didn't see the Lord until that human factor was out of the way. As he is worshipping, he realizes his own sins and confesses, "I am a man of unclean lips" (Isa. 6:5 NIV). Out of his powerful worship experience, Isaiah hears his call and says, "Here am I. Send me" (Isa. 6:8 NIV).

It happened to Peter, James, and John at the Mount of Transfiguration. They encountered the presence of God and never wanted to leave. But Jesus brought them back down from their mountaintop experience, because he had a calling in the earthly realm of human needs. In worship we encounter the holiness of God and experience it as our reality.

It happened to Paul on the Damascus Road (see Acts 22). He encountered the presence of God, and nothing in his life was ever the same afterward. The blinding presence of the Lord brought him to his knees and yielded his spirit to do the work of Christ.

It happened to me, too. The air in the sacred space called church was pregnant on that Sunday. I had returned to the church that I knew as the church of my great-grandparents. Only now my husband and son accompanied me. I walked in and the air was so expectant that I had to hold on to the pew to keep from falling. It was hard to stand. My body began to shake and I abruptly pushed our toddler into the arms of my husband with "You hold him. I can't." I sat down and held on to the pew until my knuckles were white. When the invitation was given by the pastor at Bethel AME Church in Baltimore, the man who is now Bishop John Richard Bryant, it felt as though it was all I could do to keep my body from being thrown out into the aisle and down to the altar.

I went home with a legion of questions. What was that? What was happening to me? Something was going on. "Did you see it? Couldn't you feel it?" I queried others who had been in that pregnant atmosphere. I decided I needed to come back until I found out what it was. What I eventually discovered was that my experience had nothing to do with an *it*, a *what*, or a *something*. It was *Who*, and my life hasn't been the same since.

STEPPING-STONES

1. Develop a starting point for worship or a means to increase the time and attention you devote to praising God. For example, if you attend church sporadically, commit to a 10 percent increase, either on Sunday or another day during the week.

2. Commit to spending more time engaging in the celebration of God's power and dominion over the circumstances of your life. Establish a regular time of private worship each day or during the week. If you

already engage in worship at home, expand your time by 10 percent through prayer, praise, song, adoration, confession, or meditation.

3. Read Psalm 96. Take one verse and live with it for a week, allowing it to become an affirmation of the command to praise and worship God. For example, the first verse: "Sing to the LORD a new song; sing to the LORD, all the earth" (NIV). You can make it an affirmation by saying: "I will sing to the Lord a new song; I will sing to the Lord, all the earth!" There are enough verses to do at least three per week.

4. Create time and space for worship.

5. Your home, your car, your church, and any other space you occupy should be a place worthy of giving God worship. You may devote a corner or a chair in your home for worship. The space doesn't have to be fancy or large, but it should be regarded as sacred.

6. Understand what worship looks like for you.

7. To worship means "to fall on your face or bow down" and the word *worship* is found more than 170 times in the Bible. You do not have to literally fall down, but your spirit should be postured in humility, recognizing God as the all-powerful Creator.

8. Worship in different ways (see Psalm 96). Worship with music (v. 1); with proclamation (v. 2); by giving God glory (v. 8); by bringing an offering (v. 8); by coming into his courts (v. 8); by living holy lives (v. 9); and by witnessing for God (v. 10).

9. Expand your worship practice:

   ◦ Set aside a few moments each day to give honor and praise to God.

   ◦ Look for opportunities outside the regular worship schedule of your local church to worship: with your spouse, with friends, or privately in your home.

   ◦ Discover different ways to worship God—song or hymn worship, praise or liturgical dance worship, musical instrument worship—and try them.

   ◦ Worship with believers who are not members of your church: nursing home residents, prison or juvenile facility inmates, hospital staff and patients, people in substance abuse recovery centers; or prior to a special event—such as a baby or bridal shower, a birthday or anniversary celebration, the return of a serviceman or -woman from the armed forces, or when a college student returns home.

Explore

Take my yoke upon you and learn from me, for I am gentle and humble in heart, and you will find rest for your souls.

MATTHEW 11:29 NIV

We are a small group with a big heart trying to make a huge difference in our world the best way we know how. After all, that's what Jesus told us to do.

DAVE PARKER, SENIOR PASTOR,
EASTSIDE CHRISTIAN FELLOWSHIP

Sometimes God meets us in solitary places and sometimes God provides a safe environment to grasp the promises of God while shedding guilt and shame.

I learned the importance of having that safe environment to foster spiritual growth while leading a women's support and ministry group at my church. The Circle of Love was a safe place for women to gather to seek biblical answers for daily issues and extraordinary challenges.

The rules of the circle were simple: Everyone can share. Everyone is heard. Everyone is valued. Together we seek the Lord. And finally, what is shared in the Circle stays in the Circle.

One of our most active and engaged members was April. When the Circle of Love began, she was one of the first members. She was a vibrant participant and an encouragement to the other women in the group, wrestling with a variety of concerns from doubt to diapers, men to menopause.

Suddenly she stopped coming to the Circle and to church. She told her family she was no longer interested in God, God's church, or God's people. What we didn't know at the time was that many years prior, a favorite cousin had abused April as a child. It was an excruciating experience that continued for several years, from the age of nine until puberty. Her cousin had gained the confidence of her parents and capitalized on the little girl's love of music. He'd take her to concerts, with her parents' permission, and in the dark of the concert hall, explore places of her body she wasn't fully acquainted with. By the time April hit puberty, the predator had groomed another victim.

I later found out that the infamous favorite cousin and his new wife had recently become members of our church. April no longer felt safe in worship, nor did she feel she could remain in the group, especially when we did integrity checks, querying each other to ensure we were being honest with ourselves and with other group members.

A few of the women did an intervention. They went to April's home and confronted her about her sudden nonparticipation. In a flood of tears and shame, she finally shared her childhood trauma. Her Circle sisters helped her report her abuser to her family and to authorities. She found her voice and emerged from victimhood surrounded by a sea of safety and security.

Sociologist Abraham Maslow identified safety as one of the most basic of all human needs. This makes sense, because if we don't feel safe, all the other things around us are really not important. Think about it—how important is living in a million-dollar home if you don't feel safe living there? We need a safe place to live, a safe place to love, a safe place to worship, and a safe place to explore. Are you safe where you live?

A Safe Place to Explore

You are more likely to engage in exploration if you feel safe while doing so. You are more likely to consider going on an African safari if you feel you will be safe on the journey. You may open yourself to exploring God's Word and its very personal application in your life when you have a safe circle in which to do so.

Small-group Bible study is designed as a safe and intimate setting to explore God's Word as you discern its application to your life. In this sacred space, you can find a loving group of fellow learners who will understand, empathize, love, challenge, and explore together.

In cell groups, like Sunday school or new member classes, we can stop the class leader and say, "I don't understand that," or we can share a testimony or an experience we had with the issue being addressed. There's no place for that in worship. Through group study we gain new and broader perspectives, because we are sharing with a group that has had experiences and spiritual journeys that differ from our own.

Small-group study is much more pivotal to our faith journey than simply reading the Bible. As believers share in the Word, trust develops within the room, and we tend to feel free to discuss issues with which we struggle and to receive enlightenment, encouragement, and empathy from other learners. We can talk about the struggle with getting a divorce. We can tearfully reveal the doctor's dire prognosis. Other class members will empathize as we share the frustrations of providing quality elder care to an aged parent. We can get advice about how to deal with an ethics issue on the job.

We live in challenging times, and at the same time we are privileged to live in times of great opportunities. We need to know how to relate in today's world, because there are so many blurred lines and crossed moral boundaries regarding how we should live. Believers need biblical knowledge and understanding to live for God in a world that increasingly dismisses the very existence of God.

I lead a group of clergy and lay leaders to seek biblical answers for public life and private challenges. The rules are the same as those we held in the Circle of Love. What is critical to the clergy group is the willingness to seek community within small-group ministry. It is a place where we connect and engage in meaningful conversation while receiving coaching from the Word of God.

Each of us brings a teachable spirit and leaves preconceived notions at home. When a respected person points out an area you need to grow in or grow beyond, you need a teachable spirit to receive the truth and achieve optimal growth.

It helps sometimes to share things with fellow Bible students, especially issues you are having trouble confronting. If you can't say it, the truth may be hard to face. If you can't face it, you may have a hard time offering it to the Lord to fix it. Armed with a teachable spirit, however, you can receive the truth in love and move toward a higher level of growth. Like the disciples, we should be willing to say, "Lord, teach us..."

Biblical Roots of Group Study

The practice of studying God's Word in groups can be found in Deuteronomy 31:12–13, when God said to Moses: "Call them all together—men, women, children, and the foreigners living in your towns—so they may hear this Book of Instruction and learn to fear the LORD your God and carefully obey all the terms of these instructions. Do this so that your children who have not known these instructions will hear them and will learn to fear the LORD your God. Do this as long as you live in the land you are crossing the Jordan to occupy" (NLT).

In Acts 22:3, Saul shares that in his youth he was taught the Law by the great teacher Gameliel, a leading authority in the Sanhedrin in the early first century CE. We know little about Jesus' childhood prior to age twelve, but he most likely received instruction from the rabbis at the local synagogue.

In the 1500s, Martin Luther established a number of Bible study classes and Sunday schools in Germany devoted to the study of biblical catechism, singing the praises of God and the great duty of prayer.

Other Christian education pioneers established opportunities for small-group learning in various parts of England. The Sunday school movement that most resembles our structure today grew out of a need to equip and prepare people.

The Sunday school concept was begun in 1780 in Gloucester, England, by publisher Robert Raikes, as a means of keeping children off the streets on Sunday. In the next century, formerly enslaved Catherine "Katy" Ferguson did the same for children living in New York. Although she was illiterate, Ferguson was relentless in establishing opportunities for children to gain literacy skills and Christian education.

Sunday schools were also the way many enslaved and formerly enslaved African Americans learned to read. After

Emancipation, many freed blacks desired to have literacy skills to enhance employment opportunities and so they could read the Bible. The by-product of this approach was reaching people for Christ and preparing them for life changes. Adults today need the caring community of a small-group Bible study class to help us live better lives.

Time for a Change?

If you're not a Sunday school goer, maybe it's time to make a change. If you're going but need to step up your attendance or participation, get ready to do it now! A Bible study fellowship has the capacity to change your life.

After studying the Word of God, Josiah realized that he and his people had become comfortable with their evil. They were living outside of God's law and had infused all sorts of pagan practices into the temple. King Josiah said, "It's time for a change!"

Out of ignorance, God's people had begun compromising their worship of Yahweh with other influences. We can easily pull away from doing God's will if we don't know God's Word. When we lose touch with the Word, decisions may become morally fuzzy. What was clearly wrong once may begin to seem okay when we become fuzzy on God's Word.

For many Christians today, the Word has been around for a while but has been set aside. You can do like Josiah and fall in love with it again and watch it give you a new determination.

Everyone Needs a Bethany

Who doesn't enjoy lively conversation centered around interesting topics with good people? Jesus certainly did; why shouldn't you? Imagine participating in a Bible study group that loves and ministers as Mary, Martha, and Lazarus did at Bethany. If you long for this type of loving fellowship, consider engaging in learning opportunities at your church through a Sunday school class, weekday or night study/fellowship, or small-group Bible study, either as a student or as a worker. By studying the same issues from a biblical perspective, class members build relationships that help to support each other in the discipleship journey.

I vividly remember how the Circle of Love Bible fellowship class at Payne Memorial in Baltimore evolved from a diverse group of women who were dealing with similar issues to a cohesive group who grew from pew members to ministry leaders. Over time a supportive bond of trust was developed. What was shared in the room stayed in the room. Many of the women shared from the heart; others listened quietly as they absorbed with empathy what the others had lived through.

Through that group we all experienced what it meant to participate in a fellowship of genuine agape. Some class members enjoyed an abundant series of victories while others endured rather horrific experiences. As they told their stories, we all cried genuine tears of empathy and mutual sorrow, and we rejoiced as they made progress to live in wholeness despite what they had endured.

That class was our Bethany. No one had to worry about ulterior motives or hidden agendas. There was no judgment. The room was filled with equals—sisters in the faith, united by our common bond to explore the Word of God and apply it to our lives.

Every believer needs a Bethany. Small-group Bible study is an impactful way to arrive at your spiritual place of respite. You may have every verse of the Bible committed to memory, but you still can benefit from sharing your joys and sorrows with fellow believers. In the intimacy of fellow Bible learners, you can ask, "Is it just me or is everyone else reading this differently?" There you can hurt and you can heal. You can laugh and you can cry. You can question and you can confirm.

Who's Your Barnabas?

Your retreat/advance to your spiritual Bethany can be greatly facilitated by the presence of an encourager. Some people have the gift of encouragement, and Barnabas demonstrated this attribute in the book of Acts. He was a relative of evangelist and Gospel writer Mark, either a cousin or an uncle (see Colossians 4:10), whom he would also mentor.

The name Barnabas means "Son of Encouragement." This follower of Christ was so gifted at lifting up others that fellow believers no longer called him by his given name, Joseph. Perhaps his most significant contribution was the way he encouraged Saul by validating his ministry to the Apostles, who were extremely skeptical of the Roman Pharisee's claim of conversion. They could hardly be blamed for having doubts. Saul had a notorious reputation for his relentless persecution of Christ followers. Suddenly, he claimed to be one of them. Yeah...right.

Had Barnabas not stepped in and vouched for Saul (see Acts 9), his ministry might never have taken off and many of the New Testament churches he planted never instituted.

Barnabas had accepted Saul's conversion as authentic, and he was willing to extend himself and his reputation to encourage the Apostles to accept the former Pharisee into the fellowship of believers. On the strength of Barnabas's endorsement, Saul was able to witness in Jerusalem and move freely among fellow believers.

Every believer will have a time when life's challenges can weaken our faith and cause us to doubt our purpose or God's plan. Saul was a highly educated man. He knew the Law in its every application. But he still needed someone to encourage him. No matter how educated we are, no matter how long we've been in church, no matter how long we've been studying the Bible, everyone needs an encourager to tell us to "keep on keeping on," even when we seem to be in a hopeless situation.

Everybody Needs a Balance

Sometimes you need a Barnabas, someone who sees your potential and agrees with it. Sometimes you need to *be* a Barnabas. Your kindness and your expressions of encouragement and concern to others can be a powerful incentive for them to attend small-group study.

We grow according to the encouragement we receive, but we also grow as we uplift and inspire others in their spiritual walk. And the longer you walk in faith, how wonderful it will be to look at the lives of those you've encouraged and know that God blessed you to share in their growth as they blossom. It's like looking at a field of tulips blooming in spring. They are even more beautiful when you realize that you had a part in planting them, fertilizing them, and nurturing them while they were still bulbs growing underground.

Extreme Makeover

People like transformation stories. In the last two decades, no less than three dozen television programs have featured the progress made through intentional efforts to change someone or something. *Extreme Makeover*, which first aired in 2002 and ran for five years, featured two candidates whose looks were changed in an effort to transform their lives and give them the impetus needed to make their dreams a reality. A number of other shows followed along the same basic premise—*Extreme Makeover Home Edition*, *The Biggest Loser*, *Extreme Weight Loss*, and even *Divine Restoration*, about making much-needed renovations at small churches.

We like seeing people and places formed and shaped to reach their highest potential. Remodeling stories warm our hearts and inspire hope—for a better world, for a better self. When we read the Word, we have an opportunity to take a good look at how closely our lives are aligned with God's blueprint.

In 2 Chronicles 34, a sixteen-year-old King Josiah grew deeply committed to seeking the God of his ancestor, King David. For the next few years, he set about returning Israel to being a godly nation. In the twelfth year of his kingship, he began to purify Judah and Jerusalem, destroying all the pagan shrines and the carved idols and images. He was relentless in his determination.

Israel needed an extreme makeover. Their discovery of the Law completed their quest to turn the nation around. God's Word was their blueprint to guide them to properly follow God's commands. Imagine what it must have been like for Josiah and the temple priests, trying to piece together what it means to be faithful to Yahweh before they found the sacred scrolls. They had nothing to confirm their beliefs, because they were missing the Word.

So many Christians are like Israel during Josiah's initial efforts at an extreme makeover for his people. They attend church and do all the things they believe are right without knowing the blueprint, because they don't have the assurance of knowing God's Word for themselves.

What Does Your Bible Say About You?

Respected nineteenth-century preacher Charles Haddon Spurgeon reportedly said, "A Bible that's falling apart usually belongs to someone who isn't." A Bible that has been used thoroughly usually is not very attractive, but its condition is a telltale sign of consistent use. A Bible with worn pages is a beautiful thing in the sight of God, because that means that its owner has been poring over its contents repeatedly.

Whether you use a printed Bible or an app to read electronically, what does your Bible look like? Can someone tell you're in good shape because your Bible is in bad shape? The high call of discipleship means learning God's Word with passion and purpose. It means not entrusting what you believe to a thirty-minute sermon on the occasions when you make it to church.

The Bible uses dozens of Scripture passages to confirm itself as God's Word and lay forth our responsibility to be knowledgeable of its contents, like these:

- "This Book of the Law shall not depart from your mouth, but you shall meditate on it day and night, so that you may be careful to do according to all that is written in it" (Josh. 1:8 ESV).

- "With my whole heart I seek you; let me not wander from your commandments! I have stored up your word in my heart, that I might not sin against you" (Ps. 119:10–11 ESV).

- "Your word is a lamp to my feet and a light to my path" (Ps. 119:105 ESV).

- "But he answered, 'It is written, "Man shall not live by bread alone, but by every word that comes from the mouth of God"'" (Matt. 4:4 ESV).

- "For whatever was written in former days was written for our instruction, that through endurance and through the encouragement of the Scriptures we might have hope" (Rom. 15:4 ESV).

- "All Scripture is breathed out by God and profitable for teaching, for reproof, for correction, and for training in righteousness, that the man of God may be competent, equipped for every good work" (2 Tim. 3:16–17 ESV).

Taking your faith journey to a higher level is a big deal. It begins with the small step of a commitment to explore what God says in the Word with a body of believers who are also dedicated to this knowledge. Studying alone is good, but taking your faith higher means reaping the benefits of small-group Bible study. If you're taking on the challenge, you're ready for an extreme makeover, this time from the inside out.

STEPPING-STONES

1. Open your mind to rethink your attitude about Sunday school, which is actually small-group Bible study. Consider how it can direct you toward right

thinking about life, which produces right actions in life. Look at participating in Sunday school as an opportunity to help you live according to the high calling of Christ.

2. Before venturing into a new class, carefully and prayerfully consider the cost—time, attention, energy, study, prayer, participation, innovation, and execution.

3. Find out about group Bible-learning opportunities at your church or in your community. Get excited and find others who will share in your enthusiasm.

4. If you can't find a class to get excited about, prayer- fully consider whether you may be the one God is calling to help initiate, grow, and maintain a new Sunday school or small-group ministry.

5. Find ways to get others in your home, family, or neighborhood involved in Sunday school or group Bible study.

6. Share lesson highlights during the week with people who are open to learning more.

7. Use your class as an outreach opportunity to show love to people in your church and community who are dealing with personal challenges.

8. Look for ways to use technology to share lesson truths with others. E-mail lesson outlines. Use video class interactions to share online or send discs to infirm members.

9. Think about the adults who can benefit most from Sunday school. Remember, parents will bring their children to Bible study, but children don't always have the option to bring their parents.

10. Consider starting a topical, short-term study to address a special concern—divorce, chronic illness, caregiving, financial planning, etc.

Give

For where your treasure is, there your heart will be also.

MATTHEW 6:21 NIV

It's not how much we give but how much love we put into giving.

MOTHER TERESA

Research has revealed that spending money on others actually makes us happier than spending it on ourselves, and that giving to others can actually make us healthier. "Every great moral and spiritual tradition points to the truth that in the giving of self lies the discovery of a deeper self," said Dr. Stephen Post, professor of preventive medicine and bioethics at Stony Brook University School of Medicine. What powerful reasons to give! But giving goes deeper than that for Christians. Our giving is vitally connected to our identity in Jesus Christ.

The Bible has much to say about Christians and money. In fact, God's Word contains more than two thousand verses on the subject. Time and again, Scripture associates our money with our commitment and relationship to the Lord.

The early church members helped one another and invested in what God was doing through giving (see Acts 4:32–37). They didn't feel their possessions belonged to them, but rather to the larger community of believers. Barnabas, for instance, sold a field he owned and brought the money to the Apostles. Members brought all they had to the church so that they could share with others. They provided for widows (see Acts 6:1). They also provided for those who had been persecuted because of their faith, including Peter and Paul.

Churches demonstrated a similar kind of collective support during the Civil Rights Movement of the 1950s and 1960s. Many congregations gave to help provide bail money for protesters and freedom riders. Many who could not risk losing their livelihood by participating in the movement directly gave to support those who could.

Throughout its existence, the Black Church has served as the epicenter of philanthropic efforts in the black community, quite possibly because its mission has broadly included sociopolitical concerns affecting the least and the lost. The Church has been the voice of those who could not speak on their own behalf, so many have been moved to contribute to its sustenance, including nonblacks and nonbelievers.

The Amazing Generosity of the Human Spirit

Giving inspires the human soul. Giving can spread joy, impacting and motivating others with the spirit to share and help others, especially during times of devastation and loss.

After an epic earthquake and devastating tsunami, the people of Japan struggled to put their lives back together. We had all watched with horror as the earth shook and a thirty-foot wave destroyed everything in its path. We mourned with those who lost loved ones or lost everything. We also celebrated as miracles happened—loved ones were found; a baby was pulled from the rubble; someone was found alive after days in darkness.

What inspired me most was how Japanese citizens responded to the tragedy. Near the earthquake's epicenter, warehouse workers offered survivors free coffee and soda. They shouted, "Help yourself! Take what you need," as they placed provisions on the sidewalk. Others reported that some supermarkets lowered prices so people could purchase food. People in other areas took food to those living in shelters. There were no reports of looting. In the face of such devastation, they were holding on to their moral resolve.

When Hurricane Katrina hit Louisiana and Mississippi people around the world responded to the crisis. I was most inspired by our church members in the states of Tennessee and Kentucky, the Thirteenth Episcopal District of the AME Church, where I served as their episcopal servant. People gave out of their abundance and their need to fill eleven trucks with nonperishable items, including clothes, diapers, water, and toiletries. They gave hundreds of gift cards from retailers so the displaced and their families could purchase new clothes and other items.

Generosity of the human spirit encompasses more than monetary contributions. Depending on the circumstances, giving can include time, attention, compassion, concern, or whatever you have on hand.

The warmth that generosity inspires was amplified in Haiti after a devastating earthquake, and in South Carolina at Mother Emanuel AME Church, where nine members, including Pastor Clementa Pinckney, were murdered, and at Orlando's Pulse nightclub, where forty-nine people perished and many more were injured at the hands of a lone gunman.

God calls us to a higher level of moral resolve to reach beyond ourselves to give, sharing out of our abundance or lack, to help others survive personal and public tsunamis.

Grow in Giving

God has designed the human spirit so that small change is more effective for sustaining lasting change. In addition, minor lifestyle adjustments present a good opportunity for measurable success fairly quickly, and that can encourage us to stay with what's working.

Your growth in most areas of your life is probably reminiscent of the steady advancement of the tortoise that eventually wins the race over the rabbit. This kind of slow progression happens for many people in their worship through giving. As believers grow in their relationship to Christ, they also grow in their understanding of their responsibility to give in response to God's goodness.

Jesus told his disciples to take the good news to the world, and that costs money. Perhaps that was why Jesus spoke more about finances than about heaven. Through his teachings on money, Jesus reminds us that our heart can be found wherever our treasure is. Those powerful words reveal a simple measuring stick by which to determine what we value most.

If your heart is in rearing your children in the best possible environment, then your treasure likely goes toward paying for food and clothes, and perhaps even private school tuition and field trips. If your personal health is where your heart is, your treasure might be invested in a gym membership and healthy foods that includes lots of fruits and vegetables. If your heart is in an impressive wardrobe or travel to interesting places, a quick review of your debit or credit card will confirm that.

I received a text from an old friend that read "I'm finally debt-free!" Her credit card bills were finally down to zero. It was a big deal and I congratulated her. People who have lived under mounting credit card debt and escalating interest charges can truly appreciate what it means to be debt-free.

If you're unsure where your heart is, check your bank and credit card statements. You resource your priorities. Do any of your means go to support church ministries or service programs? Is any of your time given toward community service or even helping a neighbor? What about your talent? Are you mentoring others to teach them what you know? Do you use your gifts to expand God's kingdom? Answer these questions and you will find where your heart is.

Jesus said it is impossible to serve two masters. "No one can serve two masters. Either you will hate the one and love the other, or you will be devoted to the one and despise the other" (Matt. 6:24 NIV). It's hard to tithe when you're overextended in revolving credit payments. It's hard to be free to give to worthy causes when you have a mountain of bills weighing you down. A good budget will help you identify your revenue and expense needs. Tithing or consistent measured giving unto the Lord will help you take care of your needs, finance your wants, and bless others.

A Heart to Give

In the United States, the donors who can least afford to give usually contribute the greatest percentage of their income. The bottom 20 percent of American wage earners give a greater percentage of their annual income than do those in the top 20 percent income bracket. Americans at the base of the income pyramid—those in the bottom 20 percent—donated 3.2 percent of their income to charitable causes. (Ken Stern, "Why the Rich Don't Give to Charity," *Atlantic Monthly,* April 2013.)

We find models of both kinds of givers in the Bible. First, Jesus praised the poor widow who generously gave the two mites (see Mark 12) as an offering. Conversely, he had hard words for the rich man who refused to share anything with poor Lazarus (see Luke 16). More than once, the Bible affirms that when it comes to giving, God looks at the heart. God's people are challenged to be a blessing to others as God has abundantly blessed us.

Whether you are giving time, talent, or treasure, attitude in giving is critical to its reception by God. The Lord desires gifts that are given with a joyful and loving heart (see 2 Corinthians 9:7). God delights when we give happily, filled with praise that we are able to offer our gifts. The Lord has no need for angry or miserly giving—whether in service, in praise and worship, or in offerings.

In his second letter, the Apostle Paul impressed upon the Corinthian Christians the need for a joyous attitude toward giving. He had urged them to help the believers in Jerusalem and explained that he wanted them to give in ways that were pleasing to the Lord.

Jerusalem believers had fallen on hard times due to persecution. Many Christians there had been arrested and had their personal possessions confiscated, so the Apostle had appealed to the Corinthians to help. By contrast, the Corinthian Christians were in solid financial condition.

To help the Corinthians understand the impact of their giving, Paul told them about how the Macedonian Christians were able to give by God's grace. The Macedonian believers were experiencing persecution and poverty, yet they were moved to give beyond what their circumstances deemed possible. They gave joyfully, despite their circumstances.

It may seem incongruent that poor people could give richly, but their giving was based on God's calculation in God's economy, which is fair to all. God's plan of support for the church and its ministries—tithing—is a fair plan that requires 10 percent of all givers.

Like the widow with the two small coins, the Macedonians gave beyond their human ability, even exceeding Paul's expectation. In fact, the Macedonians had insisted that they be allowed the privilege of giving to their fellow believers in Jerusalem.

The Macedonians were less financially able to give than the Corinthians. But they were inspired to give generously because they first had given themselves to the Lord. When we first give ourselves to God, pleasing God becomes more important than anything else. Our treasure and our heart become aligned.

Paul reminded the Corinthians of the greatest motive for giving—the grace of our Lord Jesus Christ. Out of love for humanity, Jesus left the wealth of heaven and became poor. Just as he exhibited such depth of love, the Corinthians were to demonstrate such affection to others.

The Corinthians also needed to exercise compassion and generosity, because the time could come when the circumstances would reverse. Whether in abundance or in lack, what was required of the Corinthians also would be required of the

Jerusalem believers so that there would be equality. All believers were held to the requirement to give joyfully.

Zacchaeus learned the principle of being joyous and generous in giving after his encounter with Jesus. The Messiah loved him into understanding stewardship (see Luke 19:1–10). After his encounter with Jesus, he offered to give back what he had unfairly taken from others. Additionally, he offered to give half his wealth to the poor and repay fourfold anyone he had cheated.

Zacchaeus transitioned from being a vigorous collector of money to a generous giver. Jesus informed Zacchaeus that his commitment to change his ways showed "salvation has come to this home today" (Luke 19:9 NLT).

By calling Zacchaeus a son of Abraham, Jesus reminded him that he was a child of promise—one of God's chosen people—and he needed to live accordingly. Jesus restored him to the family of God.

Because Jesus extended love rather than judgment to Zacchaeus, his outlook on life and on his finances was changed. Perhaps for the first time in his life, the diminutive tax collector considered the needs of others and how his occupation had impacted them. Through Christ he found something more precious than money—the unconditional love of God.

Imagine how kingdom work would be enhanced if every believer was as committed as Zacchaeus to total transformation! Many Christians conform to what God's Word tells them about giving, but they have not been transformed. They give, they work in ministries, and they use their gifts for the kingdom, but their efforts are motivated externally. They are not giving from the heart. These people are not cheating God, but they are robbing themselves of the joy that comes from being a blessing to the Lord.

A transformed believer prays to God, "Search me, O God, and know my heart! Try me and know my thoughts!" (Ps. 139:23 ESV). When we allow God to redirect our lives, we withhold nothing from God—not time, not talent, not treasure. That's not to say that we cannot engage in activities or spend money on things simply because they give us pleasure. Giving back to God is not intended to be burdensome, although at times it can be sacrificial. But a mind renewed toward the things of God commits to pleasing God in every area of life.

As your life is transformed, so are your giving and your service. The more you give, the more you are transformed. This process continues to evolve, much as the amalgam of faith and service described by Salvation Army founder William Booth: "Faith and works should travel side by side, step answering to step, like the legs of men walking. First faith, and then works; and then faith again, and then works again—until they can scarcely distinguish which is the one and which is the other."

Challenge yourself to experience the transformation that comes through receiving and accepting the unconditional love of Christ. As you continue to give generously in service to God, it will become such an integral part of your life that there is no separation from faith. You will live with a giving attitude. You will serve with a generous attitude, always searching for more ways to please God.

Ready, Willing, and Able to Give

Have you ever received a gift from someone who did not appear to be happy to give it to you? Did you feel good about receiving what the person gave you? There is a profound connection between one's giving and one's spiritual welfare.

Giving may be planned and structured, such as God's plan for tithing (see Malachi 3:10 and 1 Corinthians 16:2), but there are many ways to give. Giving may be an act of love done on the spur of the moment, like when the woman anointed Jesus' feet (see Matthew 26:6–13).

It's good to give generously. God looks at the heart more than the gift. Offerings given to impress others do not move the Lord. Furthermore, no one who is loath to part with their resources should make offerings to God. God is pleased when we joyfully give back a portion of what we have been blessed to receive. Members of the Body of Christ should view their ability to give as a blessing and a joy.

Paul used metaphors from agrarian culture to explain a divine principle of giving. A farmer would not expect to reap a great harvest from sowing only a few seeds. The same principle applies to giving. The Apostle also gave believers a promise regarding their giving: "Don't be misled—you cannot mock the justice of God. You will always harvest what you plant" (Gal. 6:7 NLT).

Doris Akers wrote a song that says, "You can't beat God giving." What God gives cannot be exceeded. The more you give, the more God gives in response. A cheerful, genuine giver has the heart of a believer determined to delight God. And when God is pleased, God postures the giver to have more and, therefore, to give even more.

It is sort of ironic to think that the one who gives is more blessed by the gift than the recipient, but this is true in God's economy. God will give abundantly to cheerful givers, and their material needs will be generously met (see Philippians 4:19).

The cheerful giver will disperse resources to various places, not just in a place that is familiar or convenient. Jesus asked, What good do we do if we love only the people who love us? Anyone can do that! (See Luke 6:32.) But just as a farmer scatters the seed generously to reap a great harvest, a cheerful giver will scatter many seeds about generously and receive a great harvest.

The blessings we receive back are not always monetary. Sometimes we receive blessings of peace in our homes or good health. However the return comes to us, Jesus promises that "no one who has left home or brothers or sisters or mother or father or children or fields for me and the gospel will fail to receive a hundred times as much in this present age: homes, brothers, sisters, mothers, children and fields—along with persecutions—and in the age to come eternal life" (Mark 10:29–30 NIV).

Respond with Gratitude

Giving back praise is the natural response of those who realize God's love for them and who appreciate God's value in their lives. Paul wrote to the Corinthians that cheerful, abundant giving would glorify God because of their generosity and because the Jerusalem believers would receive the sustenance they so badly needed. Everyone who heard what God had done through them would give God the glory.

Our grateful response to God's generosity is praise and thanksgiving. Likewise, we demonstrate our gratitude to those who allow themselves to be used as channels of God's blessings. In response to the Corinthians' generosity, the Jerusalem Christians prayed for them. They could not reciprocate financially, but they gave the Corinthians something they needed much more—prayer. The Jerusalem Christians prayed that God's abundant grace would be bestowed upon the Corinthians in their giving. The believers in both cities were offering the best of what they had to give to their fellow believers.

Giving Is Worship

Believers give for more reasons than because it makes them feel good. Giving is a spiritual sacrifice and an expression of worship, love, and gratitude, because everything we have comes from God (see 1 Chronicles 29:14).

In 1 Corinthians 16, Paul offers guidelines for giving: it is to be a universal practice for believers (v. 1); it is to be done weekly (v. 2); it is a personal act (v. 2); and it is something we should be prepared to do (v. 2). As we give, God will meet our needs and prosper us (see 2 Corinthians 9:6–10).

He advised the Corinthian Christians, "On the first day of each week, you should each put aside a portion of the money you have earned. Don't wait until I get there and then try to collect it all at once" (1 Cor. 16:2 NLT).

Giving back to God should be our priority so that our worship through giving is not compromised by other financial entanglements. Giving is a part of our total expression of worship and an acknowledgment of gratitude for God's goodness in blessings already received. Giving through tithes and offerings is also a means of reinvesting in the kingdom by giving back what belongs to God.

Our giving through worship is also an expression of our trust in God for our daily bread. When we put our tithes and offerings in the collection plate, we are acknowledging our trust in God to provide what we need right now. It is our way of providing for the needs of the church and its ministries right now. That means, on a practical level, I give because the church's light bill is due right now. I give because the Sunday school resources need to be supplied right now. I give because there is a mother and her children without food to eat right now.

Finally, our giving becomes a testament to our faith in God's promises regarding the future. Worship through giving is our affirmation of faith in God's pledge in Malachi 3:10: "'Bring all the tithes into the storehouse so there will be enough food in my Temple. If you do,' says the LORD of Heaven's Armies, 'I will open the windows of heaven for you. I will pour out a blessing so great you won't have enough room to take it in! Try it! Put me to the test!'" (NLT).

Our obligation for worship through giving, as outlined by Paul, can be understood as a 3P approach: periodic, planned, and proportionate. First, our giving is periodic, meaning there are established regular intervals for our giving—when we come to church. Practically speaking, however, our giving today should be on a plan that matches when we receive income. If you receive a retirement check on the first of every month, then your tithe can be paid on the first of the month.

Then, our giving is to be planned. Tithers consider their giving like any other financial obligation that must be paid. In order to worship the Lord through tithes and offerings, provisions must be available to allow your giving to be a reality. Your giving should be as much a part of your plan for attending church as the clothes you intend to wear or the Bible that you carry.

Finally, our financial worship should be in proportion to what we have received. God's wonderful plan for giving through the tithe allows for equity. It doesn't matter whether your income is $100 a month or $10,000—tithers are committed to give 10 percent of what they have received.

The Principle for Stewardship

The word *tithe* is a derivative of an Old English word meaning "tenth." In the days of ancient Israel, tithing was not voluntary giving. Old Testament Law required God's people to give a tenth of their income back to the Lord, which could include flocks, herds, or crops. In addition, God's people were required to give offerings to the Lord for the care of the temple and the salaries of the priests.

All of our stewardship is a blessed honor and privilege to give back to the Lord. A primary vehicle for doing so is through our local church.

A steward oversees the affairs and property of another person. Stewardship, then, implies that everything we have belongs to God (see Psalm 24). It's only on loan, as we live under the umbrella of God's generosity. Being a good steward means managing our resources well and using them to glorify God.

Good stewardship includes tithes *and* offerings. It includes giving our time and talent to the Lord as well. When we desire that our management of personal blessings be pleasing to God, we check ourselves and ask questions as a self-barometer. Am I giving enough back to God for all the blessings I have received? How can I reallocate my finances to give as God has asked? How can I find more time to give to God?

Honoring God's mandate to tithe our time, talent, and treasure means trusting God to make it all happen. When we invest in the kingdom, through faith God protects our seed (resources) from the Devourer, the enemy, and assists us to sustain our commitment to give and to serve more.

Leviticus expands on the meaning of the tithe—that it is holy and it belongs to God. That means we have no right to withhold our tithes from God. Those resources do not belong to us and we have no authority over them. When we tithe, we are returning to God what God already owns. That is why Malachi asks, "Will a person rob God?" (Mal. 3:8 ISV). Of course, the answer is yes. Refusing to give God what belongs to God is a form of robbery.

Some Christians believe that the New Testament releases believers from the obligation to tithe. But others disagree. Christians continue to tithe today as an act of worship in obedience to the Lord. It is a fair method because it is not equal giving but it is equal sacrifice. God makes an incredible promise to those who give to God's work. God will "open for you the windows of heaven and pour out for you such blessing that there will not be room enough to receive it" (Mal. 3:10 NKJV).

Both the Old and the New Testaments offer wisdom and insight regarding giving financially, giving service, and maintaining a general attitude of generosity.

- "Give, and it will be given to you. Good measure, pressed down, shaken together, running over, will be put into your lap. For with the measure you use it will be measured back to you" (Luke 6:38 ESV).

- "But when you give to the needy, do not let your left hand know what your right hand is doing, so that your giving may be in secret. And your Father who sees in secret will reward you" (Matt. 6:3–4 ESV).

- "Do not withhold good from those to whom it is due, when it is in your power to do it" (Prov. 3:27 ESV).

God extends a great promise to those who give. They will be blessed financially. God encourages us in the Word to be joyous, generous, and caring with our finances and with our service.

You Can't Afford NOT to Give!

Some people say, "I can't afford to give!" In reality, we can't afford not to. David said that he would not give to the Lord that which cost him nothing (see 2 Samuel 24:24). No matter what we give to God, what is left will always sustain us better than if we hadn't given at all.

We don't need to give because God needs our resources. Rather, God challenges us to make the kingdom the focus of our lives rather than money and possessions. The motives that God desires for our giving are to express our love to the Lord, please God, lay up treasures in heaven, and help reach the world for Jesus Christ.

STEPPING-STONES

1. Read Scriptures that relate to money, giving, and tithing to gain a greater understanding of what God expects from those who desire to obey God in this way.

2. Set in motion your plan for giving according to God's plan. If you're already a tither, don't just settle for 10 percent of your giving. Stretch your faith by increasing your percentage.

3. Attend Bible study sessions where giving, tithing, and stewardship are taught or preached.

4. Pray and ask the Holy Spirit to be your giving guide. Pray to give with the right attitude and motives. Remember that God loves a cheerful giver (see 2 Corinthians 9:7).

5. Be consistent with giving and tithing, even when you are absent from worship. Church obligations and ministries do not stop because you don't show up on Sunday.

6. Examine your total giving life. Keep in mind that giving and tithing are more than financial. Our mandate includes giving 10 percent of our time and talent to the Lord.

7. Look for ways to touch lives beyond church walls. Give earnest consideration to how you can give greater service joyfully. Where can you give greater service, and in what way?

8. How much of your talent are you using to further God's kingdom? Look at ways both within your church and beyond to extend your church's reach in the community.

9. Look at every area of your giving as it relates to your faith life. How much is your giving motivated by external factors? Using a one-to-ten scale, rate your level of joy in giving and then determine how much you want to improve it. Do you want to move from three to seven, or from five to eight? Determine where you want to go, and then set about the journey.

10. Read various Scriptures on giving, then compare your personal experiences with generosity. Are you experiencing the joy God's Word says will come from giving? If not, challenge your beliefs about giving so you may fully benefit from God's promises to those who give richly.

- Genesis 28:20–22
- Exodus 35:29
- Leviticus 27:30
- 1 Chronicles 29:3
- Psalm 112:5

- Proverbs 3:27
- Proverbs 11:24–25
- Proverbs 19:17
- Proverbs 25:21
- Proverbs 28:27

- Malachi 3:10
- Matthew 6:3–4
- Matthew 6:19–21
- Matthew 10:8
- Matthew 10:42
- Matthew 19:21–23
- Mark 12:41–44
- Luke 3:11
- Luke 6:30
- Luke 6:38
- Luke 11:13
- Luke 12:33–34
- Luke 21:4
- John 3:16
- Acts 4:32
- Acts 20:35
- Romans 8:3
- 2 Corinthians 8:1– 2 Corinthians 9:15
- 2 Corinthians 8:7
- 2 Corinthians 8:11
- 2 Corinthians 9:6–7
- Galatians 6:6–10
- 1 Timothy 5:17–18
- 1 Timothy 6:17–19
- Titus 2:7–8

Share

Encourage each other with psalms, hymns, and spiritual songs. Sing and make music in your hearts to the Lord. Always give thanks to God the Father for everything in the name of our Lord Jesus Christ.

Ephesians 5:19–20 erv

If you have a candle, the light won't glow any dimmer if I light yours off of mine.

Steven Tyler

Have you ever called a friend to share some good news about a sale? Those expensive suede shoes you got for 75 percent off or the great deal you got on a car. We love sharing good news, but how often are we excited to talk about the good news of our salvation? Jesus Christ is good news that's worthy to tell every day.

Whether you realize it or not, you are a living, breathing,

walking advertisement for the Lord. Every time you tell others about what God is doing in your life or your church, you are either helping someone make the decision for Christ or you are affirming their decision to stay away. Whenever you tell someone what the Lord did for you or your family, when and how your prayers were answered, or how you were blessed or helped by your church, you are marketing your faith and your church to others.

Living in the knowledge that you are a living advertisement for the kingdom doesn't mean posting Jesus signs, posters, bumper stickers, pins, or necklaces to broadcast your faith. When you live praising God for all of your blessings, it makes you constantly think about how good God is and how blessed you are. Your attitude of faith likely will elicit curiosity in others. The billboard of your spirit advertises peace, even in the midst of struggle. The message of your countenance promotes joy that has nothing to do with your circumstances or what's going on around you. When you live that way, you don't have to figure out how to tell somebody about Jesus, because it will be all in you and over you.

A gospel song that many of us grew up hearing in church says: "Said I wasn't gon' tell nobody but I couldn't keep it to myself…what the Lord has done for me." Sometimes it's hard to keep quiet about how good God is. God's blessings move us to share with others. We want other people to know about the job we got although the odds were stacked against us. We want to tell about the tumor that miraculously disappeared from the diagnostic scan. We can't keep secret how a wayward child's life was turned around or how a financial obligation was met.

We all have a story to tell, and your story is critical to God's kingdom growth and stability. In one of his last conversations with his disciples before ascending to heaven, Jesus uttered the command that we now regard as the Great Commission: "I have been given all authority in heaven and on earth. Therefore, go and make disciples of all the nations, baptizing them in the name of the Father and the Son and the Holy Spirit. Teach these new disciples to obey all the commands I have given you. And be sure of this: I am with you always, even to the end of the age" (Matt. 28:18–20 NLT).

Jesus placed no restrictions on his disciples—tell everyone, everywhere you go. His words are confirmed in Acts 10:34, which tells us, "God is no respecter of persons" (KJV). God accepts all who call on the Lord, regardless of race, gender, education, socioeconomic status, nationality, or geographical location. Nevertheless, there were times when even Jesus' disciples did not want him to spend time investing hope in certain kinds of people—women, Samaritans, Gentiles, children, tax collectors.

Sometimes we're guilty of that, too. Certain people may not hear about the goodness of God when churchgoers don't have a sense of conviction about sharing Jesus with others. We don't make room for them. Not in our congregation. Not in our community. Not in our social circle. Church people can sometimes confuse their house of worship with a social club. They develop unspoken criteria for membership.

After Jesus had convened his inner circle of disciples, the Twelve began to formulate their own ideas about who their rabbi should spend his time with. Jesus was an emerging star who couldn't be distracted by those considered unworthy of his time, like the Samaritan woman who was drawing water at the well in the heat of the day.

An examination of the text indicates that this was more than a seemingly chance encounter with the woman. John says that Jesus had to pass through Samaria, but this was not a geographical necessity, nor was it a cultural norm. Jesus went through Samaria because he had to share some good news with a woman who had not heard any for far too long. He engaged this woman, even though doing so put him at risk for defilement (see John 4:9). But no barrier was too great for Jesus to cross, which is our model for sharing the good news with others.

Had we been present at Jacob's well that day, we probably would have seen a woman nonchalantly carrying a large jug on her head, walking up a dusty road. In her face are traces of fading beauty. In her eyes is a lifetime of disappointment, disillusionment, and shame.

The village residents knew that she had been married five times and the man she was living with wouldn't give her his last name. Jesus immediately knew something was up with this woman who was coming to get water in the heat of the day. Most women drew their water in the morning, before the temperature began to rise. Can you imagine what it would have been like for her had she gone to the well in the morning with the other women from her village? The sound of the whispers and the side-eye looks would have been unsettling. She preferred to endure the scorching hot sun rather than the sweltering open scorn of the respectable local women.

When Jesus asked her for a drink of water, she tensed, probably clutched her water pot, and gave Jesus one of those "sista girl" looks. She was a streetwise woman. She'd been around the block a few times. In her experience, whenever a man asked for one thing, it wouldn't be long before he was asking for something else. With hands on her hips and her neck snapping from side to side, she retorted, "What are you, a Jew, doing asking me for a drink of water?"

Jesus was patient enough to work through her issues so that she could really hear the good news he had to tell. Sometimes people are not ready to receive the good news at the time we encounter them. Jesus modeled the attitude of patience we should have toward people until their ears and their hearts are open to hear God.

Jesus promised to give her Living Water. It's like the difference between fresh, moving water and stagnant water. Spring water is not like pond water. She had been drinking life's pond water so long that she didn't know there were other options. The offer of Living Water from which she would never thirst was good news to a woman who dragged water back and forth every day in the sweltering heat.

If anyone needed to hear some good news, this woman did. She was of the wrong race; Samaritans were considered inferior because only half their ancestry was Hebrew. And in the subculture of the Samaritans, she was the wrong gender.

And, in the subculture of the women, she was the worst female in town due to her relationships.

People are trying to find good news in things or people or circumstances that cannot give it. In the Great Commission, Jesus compels his disciples to share good news with people who need to hear it. We need to share good news with people who go from relationship to relationship trying to gain what people are unable to give. We are called to share good news with people who are trying to get what they need from shopping too much, or lying or gossiping, or from alcohol or drugs or food. We are called to share with those invested in relationships that don't give back.

So what good did it do for Jesus to share good news with this woman? She still had a tattered past. Still had five ex-husbands. She was still living with a man who was not her husband. She had the good news, but she still had issues, too. When the woman received the good news Jesus shared, John 4:28 says she dropped her pot and went to tell others about him. As the woman shared what had been told to her, excitement in the village was intensified. Many more wanted to hear from Jesus.

Sharing about Jesus should generate excitement, enthusiasm, and curiosity. When we tell others the good news, they will want to tell others. They will want to tell the story of how someone let go of a crack addiction after ten years of struggling on the streets. Someone needs to hear how God took care of a baby who was not expected to live. How the new job came just when the money ran out. There's a mother who wants to hear how God sent somebody's runaway child back home.

We live in a hurting world that needs to hear good news!

Jesus didn't care about the woman's ethnicity or her gender or her living situation. Do you share what God has done for you, or do you keep your blessings a secret? Will you defy the norm just so you can share with others, like Jesus defied tradition by going through Samaria?

Let Me Tell You What I Do Know

Some people are intimidated by the thought of talking to someone about their blessings or church or God or God's plan of salvation through Jesus Christ. You don't have to be a theologian to share the good news of how Christ changes lives. All you have to do is talk about how Christ has changed *your* life.

Making a concerted effort to share with others about faith, salvation, and the role of the local church is simpler than you may think. When you get a blessing, share a blessing. Sometimes our blessings come in a testimony. Sometimes we testify with our deeds. Saint Francis of Assisi is credited with saying, "Preach the gospel at all times and when necessary use words." Whether by word or by deed, look for opportunities to let someone know, "The Lord blessed me this week!" or "God is doing exciting things in my life!"

Sharing the good news doesn't mean using a bunch of complicated terms. In John 9, Jesus healed a man who had been born blind. When people began asking the blind man how it happened, his response was simple, honest, and inspirational: "One thing I know: that though I was blind, now I see" (v. 25 NKJV).

People who found out about what Jesus had done got so sidetracked in detail that they couldn't celebrate the miracle that had just occurred. Even his disciples were blinded by their own judgment. "Rabbi, who sinned, this man or his parents, that he was born blind?" they wanted to know. It was widely taught among the Jews of that day that God punished people immediately for their sin and that punishment came in the form of some sort of sickness or disease.

The disciples saw in the blind man little more than a theological debate. But Jesus saw someone through whom the work of God could be made known. Through the power of God, this man's life was changed forever. And the same thing can happen today when God's people stop being skeptical of the power of the gospel and share it.

What would happen if God's people everywhere stopped being skeptical of the power of the gospel? Millions of lives would be changed forever.

While the disciples and the community were belaboring minutiae, the Pharisees were attempting to escalate their case that Jesus was not from God, but rather was a sinner. They tried to gather evidence to make major charges against Jesus. He had healed a man on the Sabbath. Violating the Sabbath was more important to them than a man gaining his sight. Instead of rejoicing at the miracle, they were treating the healed man like his blessing was an unholy deed.

They were so hung up on their doctrines that they were clueless to the needs of hurting people. They were blind to the guilt they were heaping on a man whom Jesus had just made whole.

When you find someone who can heal your disease, why spend time worrying about what he did or where he went?

Is it possible that they were more in love with religion and tradition than they were with God? Are we more in love with our church than we are in love with Jesus? Taking the gospel to those who cannot dress to impress is more important than how we look.

Give the People What You Need

I was a church child. Church offered me what I wanted, but that had nothing to do with God. I'm not alone, I know. Like the Pharisees, church folks invest a lot of time in discussions about issues that have nothing to do with bringing souls to Christ. We focus on the style of worship rather than on the sacrifice of praise. We talk guitar versus organ or keyboard versus piano; traditional versus contemporary and anthems versus hymns, dress-up church versus dress-down; High Church versus Low Church.

When you are a church child and you grow up to be church folk, you are a worship consumer. For you, worship is not an offering; it's an expression based on human taste and preferences, the indulgent tendencies of our culture rather than a longing to reflect God's glory.

Jesus came among the church folk of his day bringing dreaded and despised transformation—changing the culture with a radical message, saying such things as: Hate equals murder and a lustful heart equals adultery (see Matthew 5:21, 27–28); adopt forgiveness as a lifestyle (see Matthew 6:14–15); don't pray and give only to be seen or impress others (see Matthew 6:5); pray for people you don't like and who don't like you (see Matthew 5:44); the poor in spirit are blessed, the meek will inherit the earth, and peacemakers are children of God (see Matthew 5:3, 5, 9); the first shall be last and the last shall be first (see Matthew 20:16). Those who were then first didn't receive Jesus' words as good news, but those who were last were rejoicing.

Jesus' good news upsets cultural and religious norms by addressing people you may not like or worship comfortably beside or want to serve with. Jesus commands that we preach the good news to the poor, set free those who are tangled up in cultural constraints, grant liberty to those held captive, help those who cannot see to receive or recover their sight, liberate the oppressed, and proclaim the good year of the Lord's favor!

Just like the disciples and the Pharisees, we sometimes get caught up sharing the wrong things about our faith.

The healed man and Jesus apparently were the only two who were focused on what really happened that day. Rather than being intimidated into explaining something he really didn't understand, the man explained the work of Jesus by essentially saying, "I don't know about all of that stuff y'all are talking about, but one thing I do know: Because of that man, I once was blind but now I see."

You can be like that man who was born blind. Stick with what you know. Focus on what God has done for you and for others in your life.

In this life, we will never fully understand the mysteries of God. That doesn't mean you can't believe. You don't have to be an elevator engineer and understand all of an elevator's mechanics to have faith that the one you board every day at work will take you safely from the ground floor to the top.

Sometimes we are blind to what is going on right in our midst, and in a spiritual sense, we can be blind to what God is doing so well for us—all because we are investing our spiritual energies in the petty and the sweaty and are not focused on God.

Remember this: A host of learned men, the Pharisees, were trying to ensnare Jesus by trapping the healed man in a theological corner. The man, who likely had no formal education, responded to their questions: "Whether he is a sinner or not, I don't know. One thing I do know. I was blind but now I see!"

If you can rattle off one thousand verses of Scripture, citing chapter and verse, that's great, but it doesn't make you a better Christian. Just because you can't explain theological terms doesn't mean that you don't have a testimony worth sharing. You can always tell somebody what the Lord has done for you:

- "God made a way for me when others said nothing more could be done."

- "God delivered me from the addiction that held me bound."

- "God comforted me in my grief and gave me hope for a better day to come."

You have many reasons to praise God and tell others. You have a testimony! Share with others what God has done and let them know, "God can do the same for you!"

Be a Game Changer!

You have the capacity to be a game changer in someone's life. You can tell someone about Christ and how he offers salvation to all—for eternity, but also for right now. Jesus is not just for the hereafter. Jesus wants to be engaged in our present lives.

In Mark's Gospel, the first recorded act of Jesus' ministry is making disciples—randomly walking on the shore and asking four fishermen to follow him. Jesus understood that the disciples he chose could make the connection from catching fish to catching more disciples.

Jesus showed up in the midst of Simon and Andrew and Philip and Nathanael and invited them to "come, follow me." This went against all the rules of becoming a rabbi in those days. To become a disciple of a rabbi meant going to rabbinical school, something prompted by a sense of calling and at the initiative of the disciple, never by a rabbinical appointment. But Jesus went looking for his disciples, found them going about their daily routine, and by his own authority told them to leave their nets and follow him.

Jesus calling the fishermen to ministry is radical. Another surprise was that the men actually did it! They left their familiar, traditional way of life, their heritage, and their families to follow a young rabbi named Jesus. They took a big risk but they didn't stop to count the cost. The call was too compelling.

When God meets us and calls us, are we surprised? More important, are we prepared? I certainly wasn't when God invited me to give up my highly enjoyable life and career and follow God.

But God calls ordinary people like you and me to be the church, the Body of Christ in the world today. You don't have to be particularly gifted for God to extend you an invitation to serve. You might be a rocket scientist; but you also might be a fisherman.

The big-time fishers of fish Jesus called had life experiences that helped them handle the administrative side of the fishing business. Someone had to know his way around debits and credits; another, to have knowledge of numbers handling and supply-and-demand issues; someone else dealt with staffing and personnel problems and solutions, compensation and scheduling, the ebb and flow of tides, bait, and equipment acquisition and maintenance.

God uses all of our experiences for kingdom building. Everything you've experienced in life becomes foundational to ministry. The Lord will use what you know and recalibrate it.

God will use your past and recycle it for the future. The Lord will use your base knowledge and reconfigure it for a new vocation. God will ably move you from catching fish to catching humans—to "go, teach, baptize, and make disciples" (see Matthew 28:19).

Jesus Will Use What You Already Have

A prophet in training by the name of Moses was looking for his arsenal. All God had given him was a rod in his hand. The only tools he had to engage in the risky ministry of civil disobedience were a stick and his brother. He was seeking what

God would give him to go back to Egypt to handle God's business of setting the captives free.

Moses was going up against a powerful ruler and nation. The deck was already stacked against him. He was a fugitive from the land. He was outnumbered, outgunned, and without an army to back him up. Despite everything Moses thought he needed, God answered his last question with a question: What is in your hand? (see Exodus 4:2). All Moses got to take with him to deliver a nation of slaves out of the hands of the powerful pharaoh was Aaron and a big stick. But God would use what Moses had.

You won't know how God can use what you already have until you give it to the Lord. And when you need it at your new level of service, it will be enough. Jesus will work with what you have and make it happen! So we go as if it depends on us but knowing that it all depends on God.

God will use what you've already experienced and what you already have with what you will need to do to serve this present age. What you're getting now is preparation for where God is going to take you in the future to share the gospel with others, casting the divine net to win the souls of humanity for Christ, to take the truth of God's Word to the doorstep of the hearer.

Cast your net to share the Word of God. You're able! The Lord has given you everything you need to handle the job. God has given you every gift, skill, grace, nuance, and experience, as well as dignity and integrity, even if you don't see it yet.

Christ has issued the Great Commission, and whether you know it or not, you are armed and ready. You're able because God is able!

STEPPING-STONES

1. Increase your efforts to share your positive testimony, God's Word, and good news to encourage others inside and outside the local congregation in the way of Christ.

2. Make a conscious effort to share positive statements about your faith or local congregation to one person each week.

3. Take information about your church ministries to someone who would benefit from an ongoing relationship with a faith community. Share flyers or announcements about your church's events at local businesses, stores, nursing homes, community centers, or meetings.

4. Share your story of faith and triumph as the Lord leads you.

5. Ask God regularly to show you persons who would be receptive to an invitation to church and/or to Christ. Invite at least one person each month to come to church with you.

6. Tell someone the good news about a ministry at your church that can benefit them. Helpful church

programs could include tax preparation clinics, addiction recovery, divorce recovery, caregivers support group, etc.

7. Solicit and receive prayer requests from neighbors, coworkers, family, and friends and pray for them regularly. Invite them to church and pray with them there. Ask them to let you know when and how God answers their prayers.

8. When God moves in your life in a meaningful way, be sure to share the good news with others, especially those in need of a message of hope.

9. Make a special effort to speak to visitors at your church and welcome them personally.

10. Post events at your church on social media and invite friends and connections to attend.

11. Consider needs in your community and work with your pastor and other church members to develop ministries to meet those needs.

Participate

Above all, love each other deeply, because love covers over a multitude of sins. Offer hospitality to one another without grumbling. Each of you should use whatever gift you have received to serve others, as faithful stewards of God's grace in its various forms. If anyone speaks, they should do so as one who speaks the very words of God. If anyone serves, they should do so with the strength God provides, so that in all things God may be praised through Jesus Christ. To him be the glory and the power for ever and ever. Amen.

1 PETER 4:8–11 NIV

The best way to not feel hopeless is to get up and do something. Don't wait for good things to happen to you. If you go out and make some good things happen, you will fill the world with hope, you will fill yourself with hope.

BARACK OBAMA

How do you prepare for God to do amazing things in your life? When Joshua and the Israelites were at the Jordan River, they had to get ready to possess the land that had been promised to their ancestor Abraham. For forty years, while they dwelled in the desert, they had been moving toward that promise.

Their preparation for God's promise didn't include the tasks that one might think. They didn't sharpen their swords or check their shields or pack their gear. God told them to consecrate themselves. In order to prepare to enter the land of promise, they needed to pay attention to God and draw closer. God wanted them prepared on the inside and the outside.

Our preparation for participation in God's service in the twenty-first century should be this same way. Draw close to the Lord and be prepared inside and out, as Frances R. Havergal declared in 1874: "Take my life and let it be consecrated, Lord, to thee." One of the greatest opportunities we have as Christians is to touch lives through participation in meaningful ministry that both challenges and changes us.

God Changes Our Direction

We all make plans and set goals, even in our Christian service. Sometimes those plans change as we allow God to use us. Sometimes along the journey, we learn that God had a different agenda from ours. David thought he was simply going to deliver lunch to his brothers (see 1 Samuel 17), but God had other plans. If we desire to please God, our plans must be open to change.

Dan Mazur was one of thousands of athlete-adventurers who trained to climb Mount Everest, which is twenty-nine thousand feet, or 5.5 miles, high. Everest is not known for its hospitality, especially when climbers reach "the dead zone," the place above twenty-six thousand feet. The dead zone temperature is below zero. Sudden snowstorms and blizzards make visibility impossible in the blinding snow.

Mazur trained for years to climb that peak. He handpicked the men who would go with him as part of his team. He raised money to make the trip and sacrificed a large part of his personal resources to get there. The challenge of climbing this mountain required months away from home, family, loved ones, and a job.

The day of the climb finally arrived. Things were going well. Inch by inch Mazur's team had made their way over the rocks, crags, and slippery slopes of Everest. Mazur and his two colleagues were within sight of the mountaintop. Years of planning were coming to fruition—learning about the mountain, saving money for the trip, looking for the right team to make the climb, training, sacrifice, and separation from loved ones. They had already been climbing for six weeks and reached the top just shy of his deadline goal on May 25, 2006.

The published account states that the air was clear, the morning bright, their hopes were up, and their energy was high when Mazur saw a flash of color—yellow fabric in a bleak environment on the ridgetop. He thought it was the tent of another team making the climb. He soon discovered that it was a man, precariously perched on an eight-thousand-foot, razor edge–thin rock. The man wore no gloves. His jacket was unbuttoned despite the frigid temperatures. His chest was exposed on this oxygen-deprived peak, which could swell the brain and cause hallucinations.

Mazur recognized that the man was delusional. He didn't know he was on the edge of the mountain and could plunge to his death at any moment. Mazur asked the man his name, and the man responded weakly, "My name is Lincoln Hall."

Mazur recognized the name. Just twelve hours prior, they had heard on the radio that a man named Lincoln Hall had died along the face of the mountain. His team had left his body on the slope. Cruel choice. But Lincoln Hall clearly was not dead. He had survived the night in subzero weather without protection. It was a miracle.

Mazur was faced with a choice. He could continue climbing and leave the man to the elements. He could make Hall as comfortable as possible and hope another team on the way down would escort him to safety. Or he could stop the climb and take Hall down the mountain.

If Mazur chose the latter, years of preparation would be lost. The top was in sight. The descent was hard enough without carrying the weight of a grown man. Taking Hall down the mountain immediately would not guarantee his survival. Or theirs. And they would have to abandon their dream of reaching the top of Everest. Mazur and his team turned their backs to the peak and took Hall down.

Would you set aside something you had long dreamed of in order to attempt a rescue to save someone who could not save himself? Would you turn away from your personal mountaintop so that someone else could survive?

The book of 1 Samuel tells the story of young David, who had been anointed king. But he was serving as the errand boy for his brothers, who were members of Saul's army. While he was delivering lunch and doing a wellness check on his brothers, he had to handle the giant Goliath. He had to turn away from a mundane task to tackle a giant challenge. No one else could handle him. Some things are just for you to do and no one else.

Later, when David became a loyal soldier in Saul's army, he was still anointed, but not yet appointed. He had to endure Saul's jealous spirit, even though he was anointed.

Participation Requires Preparation

Along David's journey, his experiences became the course work of preparation for his future responsibilities. On the battlefield, David was masterful at making his way to the top of a hill. Hill climbing requires strength and vigor. It takes a season of training and preparation to acquire those skills, which David gained while he was keeping his daddy's sheep.

Preparation puts you in a place that, no matter what happens on the way up, you will be ready. Preparation for effective participation takes time and involves more than sitting in a class, passing an exam, reading a book, networking with higher-ups, or sacrificing time and finances. Sometimes preparation is learning to hold your peace rather than retaliating against the Sauls in your life. Sometimes it's learning how to fetch and carry, how to serve another, follow instructions, show up on time, or finish what you started no matter how long it takes. Some preparation is learning how to handle fork-in-the-road decisions.

No matter what the Everest is in your life, there will always be fork-in-the-road decisions to make: choices between what you want and what needs to be done; between what needs to be done and what is best to do; or between what you can afford to do and what you cannot afford not to get done. Whether you lead a family, church, or community, you participate and make environmental, educational, physical, and social decisions that put people you care about at risk.

Jesus Christ had some fork-in-the-road moments. God's Word tells us that as the cross loomed on the horizon, Jesus prayed in the Garden of Gethsemane for another way to handle the situation. Jesus made his fork-in-the-road decision: "Not my will, but thy will, be done," thereby granting salvation to all humanity.

You Can Make a Difference

Most Christians want to feel that we are making a contribution to the world and to the kingdom. We all want to feel that we are contributing to the quality of everyday life. We all want to feel that what we do and what we say matters.

We want to know that our efforts contribute to the well-being of an institution, like church or organizations to which we belong. We want to feel that our expertise contributes to the excellence and execution of a ministry, that our service contributes to the welfare of someone in need, and that our presence contributes to the comfort of the lost and lonely. We all want to feel that whatever we do in the name of the Lord contributes to the kingdom and that our labor is not in vain.

Psychologists will tell you that one of the deepest desires that humans have is the drive to contribute. There is something in us and about us that compels us to want to add value to the existence of something or someone, to express ourselves creatively, to join groups and churches with a deep desire to make a difference.

Our forebears expressed that desire when they sang, "If I can help somebody as I pass along, then my living shall not be in vain." Historically, when African Americans had difficulty making a mark in the broader community, we could always make a mark in the church and in the kingdom for Jesus Christ.

It is this desire to participate in the betterment of humanity that fuels our highest personal ambitions, and our faith in Jesus that reminds us that faith without works is dead (see James 2:17). In spite of what our postmodern culture proclaims, human beings still rise remarkably above selfish interests to act, speak, and live in ways that are selfless.

The very act of participation—whether through service or in-kind or financial—adds purpose and meaning to our lives.

When we feel we have made a significant difference, we feel that our time has been well spent. And in the process, we not only feel that what we did mattered, but we also develop the sense that *we* matter.

If we for some reason lose the sense that what we gave matters, we sometimes feel lost or unfulfilled. And sometimes, if what we did failed to matter, then it may seem that we don't matter, and finally, that nothing matters in the world. When nothing matters, we back up and content ourselves with making sideline pontifications. We take up seats in the ecclesiastical peanut gallery to become pulpit watchers and pew sitters disconnected from the people and the places we desire to serve.

Participation in acts of service toward humanity is another way of giving to the kingdom. It is playing a significant part in something that will outlast you and make an impact that extends beyond you. That something could be a cause (eco-justice, climate change, dismantling the public-school-to-prison pipeline); collective action (Wounded Warrior Project or Bring Back Our Girls); or holding a significant position in the church.

Participation Is About God

King Solomon reminds us in Psalm 127 that if God is not in it, we're wasting our time. His father, King David, had come to this conclusion after settling into a new palace (see 2 Samuel 7). David had wanted to build God a house, also. God refused to allow David to build the temple but, in turn, promised David a dynastic legacy.

David dreamed of a temple for God and Solomon built it, institutionalizing the temple and its worship. David gathered the necessary building materials and Solomon supervised a massive building program that gave Israel influence, honor, and legitimacy.

Solomon's reign over the united monarchy included great highs and deep lows. His experiences led him to the conclusion that whatever is being built—a church, a career, a community center, a family, a home, a life—is a waste of time unless it is a part of God's purpose.

When you give of yourself, give to glorify and honor God, not for your own exultation. When you give to the ministry of the Lord, you are laying the foundation for God's presence and glory to fill the place. It's not about you; it's all about God.

When our service is all about God, we get out of the way and let God take charge. When what we do is all about God, all things work together for good. When it's all about God, you won't let what happened yesterday mess up what God wants to do through you today. When it's all about God, you realize that what you're building is more than what it appears externally. Rather, you are inspired by the presence of God, saying, "Lo, I am with you even to the ends of the earth" (see Matthew 28:20).

When your service is about God, what you do, build, or plan is not dependent upon the abilities of others. The capacity to build ministries and programs and buildings is given by God.

We receive the vision. God makes the provision. When God says, "It shall be," you can shake thoughts of doubt and fear from the stresses of your mind and scatter them like stars of a clear summer's night.

When your service is all about God, you can achieve the improbable, challenge the not yet, tackle the tough, and loose the faith to believe that nothing is impossible with God.

Participation Is About People

What in the world would we do without people? Human beings can be a great spring of inspiration or a tremendous source of irritation. As one person said to me, "I love church. It's the people I'm having a hard time with." Those sometimes irritating church people play a critical part in our lives, however. People are the church's strongest resource. They are the intelligence, the skill, and the energy behind the progress of a church under the guidance of the Holy Spirit.

People can make or break a ministry, or determine how successful a product or service is. No organization can thrive without people who love the Lord with all their heart, mind, soul, and strength!

I'm old enough to remember an old song Barbra Streisand sang, "People," from the Broadway musical *Funny Girl*, about people needing people. Ordinary people who need ordinary people are the most blessed people on the earth. Our churches are made up of ordinary people—tall, short, broad, thin, mature, young, and very young—because God uses ordinary people.

The church is people. Choir members are more than people in colorful robes. Ushers do more than greet people at the door, wearing their uniforms and sensible shoes as they direct congregational traffic. The church is the Body of Christ, the people of Christ. Jesus, who is coming back for the church, is not returning for bricks and mortar.

Because we are fallible human beings, we do not always recognize that we need other people. We do not always know what to do with people or how to treat them when they show up in our lives, especially when they have needs.

There were burgeoning needs among the early believers at Corinth. Apparently, there had been an ongoing conversation among the Corinthian church members about a variety of concerns, which Paul addressed against the backdrop of the gospel.

Paul's letter speaks to those who do the work of ministry—the entire congregation—not just the pastor or missionaries or choir members or Sunday school teachers. In the first-century church, seven people, wise and full of the Holy Spirit, were chosen when a particular need arose—the care and feeding of the widows (see Acts 6:1–7). Church officials did not appoint a food distribution task force to study the issue. They did not complain about who failed to rise to the occasion. They set about doing the work of the ministry (see Ephesians 4:11–12).

The pastoral leadership is charged with the task of equipping members to do what they are called to do. The members are charged with doing it.

This gives us two very important considerations regarding ministry participation. First, the people are legitimate workers of ministry. Second, every ministry is important.

The church needs people who are willing to do the work of ministry. Biblical commentator Dr. Greg Herrick notes: "The contribution of this section to Paul's argument is to affirm, against the arrogance and self-centeredness of many of the Corinthians, that all members of the body are needed, and that despite whether the 'weaker' members are convinced of their place, or whether the 'stronger' members are not convinced of the weaker person's place in the body, God is the one who has placed all the members in the body and who works with them so that there might be no divisions."

Our ultimate purpose is to glorify and exalt Christ and to lift up his people. God has given every Christian at least one spiritual gift to do kingdom work (see Ephesians 4:11–13).

Since every member of the Body of Christ is a member of the church ministry team, a large part of our first responsibility is to encourage people. Everyone needs inspiration at some time or another. When the winds of change nearly blow you over, hopelessness and despair will tell you to give up. Arrogance will tell you that you're better than that and you don't need nobody, no how.

The church needs people to minister to people who need people. As the Body of Christ, we need to remind them that God can turn a Red Sea into a superhighway. God can cause water to flow out of a rock like a river. God can burn cancer out of a body, calm storms, restore marriage, put families back together, deliver, save, justify, and fill with the Holy Ghost.

The greatness of a church is measured not by how many people come into the church but rather by how many go out in ministry. The church gathers, and then the church scatters. The church must go outside its walls to reach people who need the Lord.

As members of the Body of Christ, we are not like other people in the world. We live distinctively in the glory of God, who has given to us the Holy Spirit. The Apostle Peter tells us, "But you are a chosen people, a royal priesthood, a holy nation, God's special possession, that you may declare the praises of him who called you out of darkness into his wonderful light" (1 Pet. 2:9 NIV).

Use Your Blessings to Make a Difference

When we pray for God to bless us through elevation and God answers, that's not the end of the story. God elevates us so that we can use our blessings to make a difference in the lives of others. God doesn't bless a pastor to be a pastor for personal benefit. The flock's leader is blessed to serve, to lead, and to care for the people. Thank God for the people who are a blessing because they allowed God to use them.

Queen Esther had moved to the royal palace and was living large. She had people waiting on her hand and foot. Perhaps she thought she had achieved all that she was supposed to do—but God had a greater purpose for her ascendancy.

Perhaps she thought that being queen would be enough to bring pride and redemption to her people. And just as she had gotten comfortable with her position, Mordecai issued a challenge to her that revealed the true purpose of her blessing.

There's always a greater purpose to our blessings.

Naturally, at first Esther didn't want to jeopardize her position with her husband, the king. Mordecai challenged her to take her consciousness and her faith to another level. He wanted her to believe that God could do more than put her in a mansion and give her a title, servants, and jewels. That wasn't the end of her story.

Esther needed to use her influence to save an entire nation of people. She loved Mordecai, who was like a father, but she was reluctant to risk her position in order to get involved.

Mordecai was unsympathetic to her predicament and issued her a challenge: "Do not think that because you are in the king's house you alone of all the Jews will escape. For if you remain silent at this time, relief and deliverance for the Jews will arise from another place, but you and your father's family will perish. And who knows but that you have come to your royal position for such a time as this?" (Est. 4:13–14 NIV).

Sometimes we may wonder why God has called us to where he has called us. Even if we wonder, we can always know that it ain't just about us!

Mordecai's statement was powerful! He wanted Esther to know that being in the king's palace would not guarantee her immunity from persecution. Likewise, we need not think that we're immune from life's vicissitudes simply because of what we have achieved.

Esther could not afford a false sense of security. Mordecai challenged her, essentially saying: "You got a calling for something that's more important than you!" He wanted the young woman he had raised like a daughter to use her blessings and gifts for a cause that was lasting and would benefit someone other than herself.

Jesus warns us not to store up treasures in the things of earth, "where moths and vermin destroy, and where thieves break in and steal. But store up for yourselves treasures in heaven, where moths and vermin do not destroy, and where thieves do not break in and steal" (Matt. 6:19–20 NIV). Queen Esther's royal robes, gold jewelry, and crown are long gone. But what remains is her crown of righteousness, and the celebration that memorializes her work lives on.

There's an old song that says, "May the work I've done speak for me." The work of many dedicated Christians is still blessing others because they invested in the things that last—kingdom work.

While Esther was working things out, the Lord moved. She did all she knew to do. God prepared and paved the way for Esther to approach the king with her request.

There are times when we do all we know how and we just have to trust God for the rest. When we step forward to serve God in obedience, God will move in, clearing the path ahead.

God chooses us for participation in building God's kingdom.

Others may not see why God calls a particular person for a particular task. You may not even see what God sees in you. Moses couldn't understand what in the world God could want with him! But God knew.

Engaging in kingdom work is never easy because service is about sacrifice. Participating in ministry that builds lives and honors God is rewarding, but also challenging. Often it's lonely. We look for assurance as we forge ahead in obedience to the call, and at times it seems nowhere to be found. Hold on to God's unchanging hand. No matter what may come, we can depend on the Lord to uphold and empower us to carry out God's vision.

What service are you using your gifts to do? Because you are a believer in Jesus Christ, God has put a call on your life. Will you answer? Or are you waiting on someone else to do it?

Let God direct your paths of participation and guide you to use your giftedness in this changing and challenging world. No matter what happens, God always has an assignment for you at such a time as this.

STEPPING-STONES

1. Pray for God's guidance on enhancing the vision of small groups with which you may already be engaged

in ministry. Also, explore new small-group possibilities for meeting the needs of the people in your church.

2. Study innovative ministries at other churches and consider how a similar endeavor could impact your community.

3. Start small and build. If you keep going and don't give up, other people will join you. People like being associated with action and impact.

4. Look for ways to assist the pastor to increase participation in meaningful ministry beyond worship.

5. Invite friends, family, club members, and coworkers to participate with you in small-group ministry whether they belong to your church or not.

6. Be a welcoming spirit to those who do not belong to your church or new members when they come to participate in a group-ministry opportunity.

7. People desire to belong and to be accepted. There are also many lonely people in this modern world full of social media outlets. Small-group ministry may provide an opportunity for inclusion that chases away feelings of uselessness and loneliness.

8. Prayerfully consider whether God wants you to be the catalyst that initiates meaningful ministry opportunities for yourself and others in your church and community.

9. Devote at least one minute of daily prayer and meditation to asking God to show you a greater vision for ministry. Tell God you don't want to be a benchwarmer. Ask God to show you how to get on the team and into the game!

10. Increase your participation in meaningful ministry that leads to a mature faith in Jesus Christ.

Grow

I am the vine; you are the branches. If you remain
in me and I in you, you will bear much fruit; apart
from me you can do nothing.

JOHN 15:5 NIV

All around us worlds are dying and new worlds are
being born; all around us life is dying and life is
being born. The fruit ripens on the tree; the roots are
silently at work in the darkness of the earth against a
time when there shall be new leaves, fresh blossoms,
green fruit. Such is the growing edge!

HOWARD THURMAN

Howard Thurman, revered preacher, theologian, mystic, and educator who served as dean of the chapels at Morehouse, Howard, Spelman, and Boston universities, wrote that we are called to look always to the "growing edge." As followers of

Jesus Christ, we have an opportunity to live daily at the growing edge of our faith. This growing edge is the process of having a relationship with Jesus Christ and receiving revelation from God's Word that brings about a change in thoughts, words, and deeds. It is the place where we prioritize our lives around the Christ who is always bringing new things, new ideas, and new concepts to our spiritual awareness. The Lord is ever among us, offering us a closer walk, new revelations, fresh wind, and fire.

The growing edge is the transformation process within us. It is the evidence of our discipleship, as demonstrated by a deeper spiritual relationship where we experience the gift of God's presence.

Embrace Your Growing Edge

How do we get to the growing edge? We find it by participating in shared opportunities for discipleship, learning, and training.

In 1743, John Wesley created a three-part discipleship-training model that included "a company of people having the form and seeking the power of godliness, united in order to pray together, to receive the word of exhortation, and to watch over one another in love, that they might help each other to work out their own salvation."

The model replicated a three-strand cord about which the Ecclesiastes writer proclaims: "A person standing alone can be attacked and defeated, but two can stand back-to-back and conquer. Three are even better, for a triple-braided cord is not easily broken" (Eccles. 4:12 NLT).

Believers should lean on each other for strength in the process of spiritual growth. When we have established firm relationships with fellow Christians as prayer partners and Bible study partners and accountability partners, it fortifies our desire and resolve to live the way Christ intended.

At the growing edge of discipleship, we are able to experience the extraordinary gift of God's presence. There we are able to prioritize our lives around our relationship with God, growing daily with an increased hunger and thirst after God's righteousness.

The way to begin the challenge to grow starts by discovering where you are in your development of spiritual disciplines such as prayer, study, worship, and praise. Take a few moments to take a personal discipleship inventory. You can find many such tools in books or online.

Know Where You Are

You've probably been in a mall or large building and stood in front of a map showing the floor plan. Somewhere on the map there will be a dot, accompanied by the words "You are here." That dot is extremely important when you're trying to find your way, because if you don't know where you are, you can't get directions to where you are going. In the same way, if you don't know where you are in your faith walk, how can you chart a spiritual path to where you are going?

When you know where you are, then you begin to realize what is needed in your life to grow closer to God. When you know where you are, it can help you to navigate your way to a new or higher direction, especially when you're in a painful growing place. As you make steps to move away from a difficult place toward a place of greater wholeness and purpose, it's important to mark your way with the question, "Does this honor God?"

In Psalm 119:11, the writer says, "I have hidden your word in my heart that I might not sin against you" (NIV). When we study the Word of God to the extent that we even commit it to memory, we carry the Word with us. God's Word is a guide to help us as we travel along the growing edge.

Growing to the next level of where God wants us to be is rarely easy. Often it involves some changes and challenges. It can be a painful process. But the growing edge is where meaningful change occurs. It is where God shapes and molds us to accommodate the space God has designed for us to fill.

The growing edge we travel can be fragile, because change is taking place, much like the fragility of a baby chick pecking its way through the shell it has outgrown. This breaking-forth process can seem painstakingly slow. The chick enters its new environment slowly, pausing occasionally and acclimating to the new world in which it will reside.

When I am at the precipice of struggle, I find that this

growing edge is the place where my faith expands to meet God. While I'm out there, my faith enlarges and stretches, because I have to depend on God to help me navigate this new place.

Sometimes the growing edge meets me in prayer or in Scripture, when God puts a mirror to my spirit while I'm praying or reading the Bible. At those times it can cut me right to the heart and cause discomfort. I may not like what I see and realize it's growing time. And it's a continual process. I don't think you ever outgrow the need for a growing edge, and you never get comfortable in that space. For those reasons, it's also where you learn to stop saying "never."

When God positions you on the growing edge, you stop fighting where God wants you to go. You don't argue back about doing what God wants you to do. You accept that God's plans supersede your own, and eventually you take comfort in that fact. After wrestling with God on the growing edge of your life, you learn to relax and rejoice in God's omnipotence.

On the growing edge you find peace in living in obedience to God's will and way. As the world calls to you to be successful, God calls you to be faithful. In faithfulness and obedience to using your God-given gifts according to God's plan, you find fulfillment, purpose, and peace. You discover the person God knew was inside of you.

God knew the person inside the young shepherd boy David when the prophet Samuel was instructed to anoint him as king. God saw the capacity for great leadership. God saw in Moses a deliverer for Israel while he was still an exile herding his father-in-law's cattle. God saw in the Samaritan woman an evangelist who could spread good news to her community.

Whatever you have the capacity to become, God has already seeded in you. Your task is to recognize where you are and allow God to lead you along your growing edge. Stay with the Lord, who said in John 15, "I am the vine; you are the branches... Apart from me you can do nothing" (v. 5 NIV).

Wear Your Own Armor

After David had determined that he would fight, and defeat, the giant Goliath (see 1 Samuel 17), King Saul was concerned about this lad going up against a ruthless fighter more than double his size. "Well, if you're determined to go, let me at least give you my armor to wear when you go up against him," he essentially told David.

King Saul probably had very elaborate armor; after all, it was meant to protect a king. But when David put the armor on, he basically said, "Thanks, but no thanks." David had mastered use of the sling, which was what he would use to defeat Goliath. His aim needed to be quick and sure. Wearing a lot of armor would only get in his way.

Saul's armor was needed for Saul's battles. Saul meant well. He wanted to protect David. But David had to fight with the weapons he was gifted to use. David needed his own weapon and his own armor to fight. His armor was his faith in the Lord.

Sometimes we see someone in church who seems like the

perfect Christian, although we know in fact that there is none. Yet they seem to know the right things to say and do. We never hear them speak a cross word or show anger or frustration. They always seem to be engaged in good Christian activities. We look at them and think, "I need to be like that." We start trying to wear someone else's armor, but what we really need to consider is that God takes us and calls us—flawed and fumbling—and uses us to do great things.

God calls us just as we are. And as we accept that call, we are shaped into the mind of Christ, not the mind or actions of another human being. We were created uniquely, and that's how we render our service unto the Lord. You don't have to fit some arbitrary mold to be a disciple. So many of God's faithful servants did not fit a mold that was held by society or even by personal expectations. Even Jesus didn't fit the mold of what a messiah should look like and how he would arrive. Deborah didn't fit the mold of a judge or a general. The Creator of all has the authority to break any and all molds that confine us and restrict our ability to serve. God's call is our invitation to break the mold, because rarely does God call people to stay within their comfort zone.

God saw a mighty warrior in Gideon while he was still hiding in a winepress. While Hannah was distraught over her barrenness, God saw the son she would bear and dedicate to the Lord. Mary was a teenage virgin from humble roots, but God saw a young woman with faith strong enough to believe that God's Spirit could impregnate her. Peter was hotheaded, but Jesus saw someone who could lead three thousand souls into the kingdom (see Acts 2:41) and who had the faith to heal people as they fell under his shadow. God saw more than a religious zealot as Saul went about breathing murderous threats to the Lord's disciples (see Acts 9:1).

God, your Creator, already sees what is inside of you. Allow God to position you along a growing edge.

The Growing Edge of Discomfort

Our growing edge challenges us to stretch beyond the routine of discipleship. We can easily fall into a mundane form of following Christ. We go to church on Sunday. Choir rehearsal on Tuesday. Attend Bible study and prayer meeting on Wednesday. Missionary meeting on Saturday. We pay our tithes and offer our morning or nightly prayer. Then we start all over again the next week.

Routine and structure play important roles in faith and worship. It's reassuring to know that God desires that everything be done decently and in order (see 1 Corinthians 14:4). The tithe is God's structure for our giving. The Model Prayer is God's structure for our prayer. Every church has an order and a structure in its leadership and worship. But order and structure should not be used as tools to push out God's Spirit, which is moving us along our growing edge to greater faith and service. We should always remain open to saying yes to God.

Celebrated television director/producer Shonda Rhimes decided that her life journey should include a year of saying yes to things she would normally decline. She shares her journey in her autobiographical work *The Year of Yes.* She decided that for one full year, she would stop saying no to opportunities and say yes. In addition to saying yes to opportunities like Hollywood gatherings, she also decided she needed to consciously say yes to good health (she lost 120 pounds), yes to friendship, and yes to love.

God wants us to have a lifetime of saying yes to God's will and God's way. By responding to God affirmatively, we can experience the greater blessings, much like the Twelve did when they dropped their nets and abandoned their boats after Jesus challenged them to "follow me."

When we say yes to God, we have to trust God for where that yes will lead. Saying yes requires faith that tells God we will go and obey, even when we don't know what the end will be. Abraham is lauded for his faith because he trusted God and obeyed God's call, even though he didn't know where he was going (see Hebrews 11:8).

If we can see the end, we don't need faith. We can't halfway trust God, and God won't necessarily give us a preview of where we're going. Our job is to trust God to lead us through the uncomfortable and to guide us through the unorthodox. As we grow in faith and travel the growing edge, we learn to be certain amid life's uncertainty and tranquil during life's tests and trials.

When we are thrust into the position of the growing edge, the question of why sometimes enters our spirit: "Why me, God?" or "Why now, God?" But if we continue on the journey with God, either we will find an answer or we will find peace in the situation.

I remember asking why when our baby daughter died. She never left the hospital. We couldn't understand why she would reach the third trimester only to die. My husband and I wondered why I needed to go through seven months of pregnancy to carry a child who would not live. In the midst of that situation, everyone simply assumed I was okay and handling everything like a super Christian. But I really wasn't okay. Everybody was saying, "We don't have to worry about Vashti." But they really should have worried at the time. I didn't know that I was on the growing edge at the time. I was simply on the hurting edge.

I was on the hurting edge as I visited hospitals and held the hands of mothers as they gave birth. I was privately in pain even as I was rejoicing with them over their new arrivals. But as I kept walking along that painful growing edge, I was able to sympathize with women who lost their babies and encourage them. When I told them, "I understand," I really did. As I walked further along that growing edge, I was able to comfort grieving mothers who lost their babies and would never have an opportunity for another. I could thank God that I would have other opportunities at pregnancy, and I did. I was grateful for the opportunity to console women with empathy and understanding, but I was also grateful for second chances. As I journeyed along my growing edge, the why became less of a priority.

Why is important but can't be your main concern. In fact, when you ask why, God may even tell you, "That's my business, not yours." There are some things we are not meant to understand on this side of life.

When you're out on the furthest point of the growing edge,

you will want to let go, and sometimes you may for a while. But thankfully, God will not let you go. God will be there until you return to that place of growing, and you will take comfort in the fact that God never left you. Somewhere along the way you will realize that God was preparing you to be something more, something greater for God's purposes. The storms ravaged my weakness but unlocked my true strengths.

In Isaiah 54, God invites us to widen the place of our tents because God is about to do something. God has some blessings for us along the journey. We don't understand it all, but God does. Getting to the blessings can be a process. God had already anointed David king of Israel, but David had to fight Goliath to obtain a king's riches. We must grow into what God has for us, even though the growth process may include pain and discomfort.

Make the Most of Your Gifts

Jesus tells a parable about three servants who saw things differently. Luke's Gospel tells us Jesus entered Jerusalem followed by a crowd of both disciples and skeptics (see Luke 19:28–44). Jesus overheard them talking about what the kingdom was going to be like, so he used this teachable moment to tell them a story (to which I added my own twists): "You want to know about the kingdom, do you? Okay: There was a nobleman who went far away to be awarded his kingdom..."

Jesus said, "A man summoned ten of his slaves." The noble owned them, but he trusted them and gave them great responsibility;

nevertheless, they were his. The slaves arrived and the noble gave each of them a certain amount of money and said, "Be productive with this until I get back. Make more money!"

The nobleman returned as a king. Most likely, he had come back with a large entourage, perhaps even an army. The man who had absolute power over the slaves' lives now had absolute power over everyone's life. The new king sent for his slaves.

There's an overachiever in every crowd: the one who always raises his hand first in class; the one who always finishes her project first and then presents it to her boss in a flawless PowerPoint presentation. You know the type. Well, the overachiever slave came forward. She had multiplied what the king gave her tenfold. He was impressed and placed ten cities under her authority.

The second servant wasn't quite so ambitious, but he still did quite well. Perhaps with a grumbling look at the first slave, he handed over a return of fivefold. The king was pleased and gave the second slave five cities to rule over. We assume it continued this way until the last slave came forward. It could not have been much fun for him, watching as the others presented their earnings. If, like me, you spent more time sitting outside the principal's office than you did in class, you know exactly how this last slave felt.

The last servant swallowed the lump in his throat, stepped forward, and gave the speech he had prepared: "Your Majesty, I know that you are a harsh man who takes whatever he wants, even if it's not his. I did not want to anger you, so I took your money and hid it under my mattress. Um, here it is. The same amount that you gave me. I didn't lose a penny of it."

The poor, overly cautious servant was afraid that the king's standards were so high he would never live up to them, so he simply hung on to what he had been given. Here's where the most terrifying sentence in the story comes in. The king looked at the slave servant and said, "I will judge you by your own words!"

He continued, "You know that I take what is not mine? Then why didn't you at least put the money in the bank so that it could have made a little interest? Since you didn't even bother to do that, I'm taking it all back and giving it to the slave who made me ten times what I gave her. Get out of my sight! Those who have more will get even more, and those who have nothing will lose it all" (Luke 19:11–27).

This story parallels the kingdom of God. It is a place where the gospel is generously given in equal amounts to us all, but those who keep that gift to themselves lose it.

Isn't this what many of us, deep down, are afraid God is really like? Are we afraid that God will find our faith or our lives lacking, or that—even if we make the cut on the Day of Judgment—our friends and loved ones who aren't Christians won't be with us in heaven?

Those fears can be paralyzing. Many of us come into church Sunday after Sunday, never feeling worthy to hear the words of absolution or to share in the Eucharist. If you are barely hanging on to your faith by a thread, this parable is not directed at you. It would do a great disservice to the entirety of the Bible to use this one text to terrify you out of faith in a God of love and mercy. God says, "My grace is sufficient for you, for my power is made perfect in weakness" (2 Cor. 12:9 NIV).

God promises to never leave or forsake us (see Hebrews 13:5). God assures us there is no condemnation for us through Jesus (see Romans 8:1). We understand and interpret this parable in the fullness of Scripture, which offers comfort to those who are challenged and extends challenges to those who are comfortable.

This parable teaches us that as Christ's possessions, we have been given incredible gifts—mercy, grace, and hope—generously and without limits. The purpose of these gifts is not to keep them to ourselves. God has given these to us so that we can give to others—so we can generously forgive other people and generously care for others, so that we can heal, support, and affirm others as God has healed us.

Every believer gets something to share in God's kingdom. In Matthew's Gospel, everyone receives according to his or her ability and capability. In Luke's Gospel, all received the same thing. In either case, everyone in God's kingdom has an opportunity. No one is left out.

Whatever you have been given, determine by faith that you will expand it, because it's not what you have that matters; rather, it's what you do with what you have. One servant brought back tenfold, while another did nothing but bury what he had been given for safekeeping. How much of what you have been given is buried? Do you have dreams buried under daily responsibility? Visions concealed beneath fear and doubt?

We may choose to live like the servant who had a fivefold increase. He did half of the best. Some people live in halfway mode—they get halfway through school, they remain halfway married, or are halfway raising their kids. It doesn't matter what they're doing, it's going to be halfway. In order for a ship to come into harbor, it must dock all the way, not halfway.

The servant who increased her master's investment tenfold made the most of what she had been given. We, too, can make the most of our resources. Make the most of your gifts, time, ideas, dreams, finances, career, and your faith walk.

What the king gave his servants wasn't a test to trap them; it was an opportunity to grow. He chose each of them because he knew he was dealing with servants who had already been tested and tried. He knew they already had the tools they needed, and he allowed them to manifest their gifts before his return.

By the Grace of God

Christians have an opportunity to live daily at the growing edge within our faith communities. That is the place where we receive revelation from God's Word, which effects change in our thoughts, words, and deeds. It is where we learn to prioritize our lives around the Christ who is always bringing new things, new ideas, and new concepts into being.

The Lord is ever among us, calling us near—offering a closer walk, new revelations, fresh wind, and hotter fire. At the growing edge of discipleship, we are able to experience the extraordinary gift of God's intimate presence. We are able to prioritize our lives around our relationship with God, growing steadily with increased hunger and thirst for righteousness.

Luke paints a portrait of a Jesus who constantly challenges disciples, in both word and deed, to widen our circle of concern. Old enemies become heroes—like when the hated, despised Samaritan is portrayed in a positive light. Outcasts like lepers and blind men are recipients of God's grace.

Everywhere he went, Jesus' message was that what he has to offer is not just for a privileged few. As his followers, what we have to contribute to humanity for the kingdom's sake cannot be limited to people who look like us, talk like us, or believe like us.

Jesus challenges his disciples to give to people who don't fit and to make sacrifices that stretch our faith. To those who follow Jesus with abandon, he offers a great promise: "Truly I tell you, . . . no one who has left home or wife or brothers or sisters or parents or children for the sake of the kingdom of God will fail to receive many times as much in this age, and in the age to come eternal life" (Luke 18:29–30 NIV).

We will not lose for the sacrifices we make to serve God. So that if I am moved by the Spirit to buy groceries for a family whose cupboards are bare, even though I still have a week to go before my next payday, somehow the food in my refrigerator and the gasoline in my car will last until my next payday.

Jesus' promise means caring enough to listen to someone else's problems, even though their situation seems trivial compared to your own circumstances. But somehow God grants you the peace to endure your situation until a better day comes.

A Disciple Is a Bridge over Troubled Water

Paul Simon wrote a song in late 1969 that was embraced internationally and far beyond his expectations. Reflecting on the song's popularity, Simon said that he had thought the lyrics were too simple, but he later realized simplicity was the key to the success of his Grammy Award–winning composition.

"Bridge over Troubled Water" won five Grammy Awards in 1971. The song appealed to the masses because one human being was reaching out to another saying, "I've got your back when you're in trouble."

Everyone wants to know there is somebody who has his or her back, especially during the toughest times of life. Jesus calls his disciples to be bridges and bridge builders over the troubled waters of the human experience.

Disciples are bridges who stand in the gap between hopelessness and help. We can find the "whosoever" Jesus speaks of—wherever they are, whatever their condition, and whenever we can.

We are the whosoever connection Christ calls and commands to reach out to persons and show them a glimpse into the kingdom. Whosoever is the bridge that invites the world to God. Whosoever is the welcome mat of heaven extended to humanity. Whosoever issues no qualifying rules or regulations to being aided.

Max Lucado writes in his book *3:16: The Numbers of Hope* that the designation "whosoever" sledgehammers racial fences and dynamites social classes. It bypasses gender borders and surpasses the barriers of ancient traditions. The word *whosoever* makes it clear that God's grace is given to the world, without our permission or input.

As the Body of Christ, we can help build bridges over the troubled waters of those who are hurting and to those who are already doing good work in business, education, medicine, technology, and even in politics. We can participate in policy making without being used or compromised.

A bridge over troubled waters is a place of reflection and refuge. Be the bridge so that through the Word of God, the whosoever can let go of excess baggage. Be the bridge that will lead someone to take the first steps in Christ. Build a bridge over troubled waters; one that, after we have tried God, we learn to trust.

You Do Something About It

During his Sermon on the Mount, Jesus found a teachable moment to help his disciples understand what it means to follow him. When the hour grew late, the disciples attempted to distance themselves from the needs of the people. They reminded their Teacher that something needed to be done. It was late and people were hungry. Send them home, Jesus, they said.

Instead of Jesus raising his hand and calling out the benediction, he told his disciples, "You give them something to eat" (Luke 9:13 NIV). "What? You want us to do something, Jesus?" This exchange on the mountain was the first time Jesus gave them the responsibility for solving a problem. He was helping them get used to the idea that solving problems is part of a disciple's job.

They had no reason to think about serving anyone but their Teacher, not realizing that serving others was the same thing as serving Jesus (see Matthew 25:40). They were too preoccupied with the tasks of Jesus' ministry to engage in an activity as mundane as feeding people. The story, which is found in all four Gospels, does not indicate that the people in the crowd could not afford food. Nevertheless, they had nothing to eat and were situated in a remote location. They had a need. How many people would have retorted that the people could afford to go and buy their own food?

They were caught up in telling the Word and not being the Word. Like the disciples, many of us are so caught up in "the Word," whether we are preachers, teachers, deacons, missionaries, choir members, or pew sitters, that we don't have time to worry about the needs of people. In chapter 17 of his Rule of 1221, St. Francis of Assisi told the friars not to preach unless they had received the proper permission to do so. Then he added, "Let all the brothers, however, preach by their deeds." No disciple is too great or powerful to babysit for a single parent who just needs to get a little time out alone, or to sit with an elderly man who tells the same stories over and over again.

In the minds of the Twelve, Jesus was the Messiah who could fix all things. What did they need to do besides follow him around? We are also guilty of waiting for Jesus to do something about the problems around us, not realizing that we are his hands and feet. As we turn to Jesus, he turns to us, saying, "What about you?"

Jesus placed the responsibility of caring for the people back onto the Twelve. They questioned how they could possibly feed so many. They had all neglected their businesses to follow Jesus, so not one had the income to buy food. They informed Jesus it would take eight months' wages to feed all of those people.

Jesus forced the Twelve to see a need they did not think was their concern. Jesus made them *own* the people's need. The disciples thought they had done enough simply by suggesting that he send them away. That was thoughtful of them, wasn't it? Jesus desires more than mere courtesy from his disciples; he requires service.

One of the amazing facts of our faith journey is what God is able to accomplish through us and in spite of us. Jesus rounds up sinful, selfish men and women of faith and molds and shapes us into instruments he can use to bring glory to God.

The vastness of human need overwhelms us, because the issues seem far too big for us to resolve, and they are. When we consider our personal resources alone, we cannot meet the need. The disciples were right. Thirteen ordinary wage earners could not possibly afford to feed over five thousand people. But our faith cannot be based on our circumstances (see Hebrews 11:1).

Have you ever questioned God as the disciples did that day? Many Christians have received a call from the Lord that causes the heart to flutter and the mind to spin: "God, you can't be serious! Do you know what you're asking me to do?"

Just as he challenged the disciples that day, Jesus confronts us with situations that appear overwhelming. The call he extends lifts us out of our comfort zones and into the faith zone along the growing edge. That day, Jesus propelled his disciples into a higher faith zone.

One Can Make the Difference

A story was shared with me about a researcher who compared the responses of children and college students by asking them what they wanted to be when they grew up. One nine-year-old wanted to be an auto mechanic or a garbageman because, he said, "I can be dirty all the time." Another child wanted to be in charge...of what? That child just wanted the power to call the shots.

The researcher then asked a group of college students what they wanted to be. Their responses weren't about being rich or famous, nor was their primary concern finding a job or getting paid doing what they wanted. The group said that they wanted to make a difference in their lifetime.

Of all the things you want to do as you journey through life, I hope you have made a decision to make a difference. You don't have to be powerful or wealthy or brainy or brilliant to make an impact on humanity.

Caesar Rodney was a Delaware delegate to the Continental Congress in 1776. Virginia delegate Richard Henry Lee had introduced a controversial resolution for independence from England. Rodney was not present during the vote, but got notice via courier that he was needed in Philadelphia immediately, as the delegates present were hopelessly deadlocked. Rodney was seriously ill at the time, but he rode the eighty miles all night by horseback through a torrential rainstorm and arrived at Independence Hall on July 2. He cast the deciding vote for his colony, adding Delaware to the successful vote that day, and the eventual unanimous vote later in July. Caesar Rodney made a difference and altered the course of American history.

Rosa Parks remained in her seat and set race relationships in a new direction. Martin Luther King Jr. marched through the streets of southern and northern cities alike, declaring, "We shall overcome," and we did.

One person can make a difference.

STEPPING-STONES

DISCIPLESHIP EVALUATION

Rate yourself regarding the following disciplines:

"Living Daily in God's Presence" (20-Point Maximum)

- Morning quiet time
  Always   Usually   Sometimes   Seldom   Never
- Evening quiet time
  Always   Usually   Sometimes   Seldom   Never
- Seek God's presence during the day
  Always   Usually   Sometimes   Seldom   Never

- Aware of God's leading presence
    Always   Usually   Sometimes   Seldom   Never
- Discipline self to the leading of the Lord
    Always   Usually   Sometimes   Seldom   Never

"Living in God's Word" (24-Point Maximum)

- Daily Bible reading
    Always   Usually   Sometimes   Seldom   Never
- Attend weekly Bible study
    Always   Usually   Sometimes   Seldom   Never
- Keep notes from study times
    Always   Usually   Sometimes   Seldom   Never
- Memorize Bible verses
    Always   Usually   Sometimes   Seldom   Never
- Attend Sunday school
    Always   Usually   Sometimes   Seldom   Never
- Share God's Word with others
    Always   Usually   Sometimes   Seldom   Never

"Praying Without Ceasing" (20-Point Maximum)

- Daily private prayer time
    Always   Usually   Sometimes   Seldom   Never
- Corporate prayer time / praying with others
    Always   Usually   Sometimes   Seldom   Never
- Intercessory prayer / praying for others
    Always   Usually   Sometimes   Seldom   Never
- Keep notes on prayer requests and prayers answered
    Always   Usually   Sometimes   Seldom   Never

- Pray throughout the day
  Always   Usually   Sometimes   Seldom   Never

"Worshipping with Others" (24-Point Maximum)

- Worship weekly at a local congregation
  Always   Usually   Sometimes   Seldom   Never
- Worship at a midweek service
  Always   Usually   Sometimes   Seldom   Never
- Invite others to worship
  Always   Usually   Sometimes   Seldom   Never
- Worship privately at home
  Always   Usually   Sometimes   Seldom   Never
- Come to church ready to worship
  Always   Usually   Sometimes   Seldom   Never
- Desire to worship in peaceful harmony with others who may/may not like you
  Always   Usually   Sometimes   Seldom   Never

"Worshipping for the Lord" (24-Point Maximum)

- Serve Christ by serving in the church
  Always   Usually   Sometimes   Seldom   Never
- Serve in at least one ministry of the church
  Always   Usually   Sometimes   Seldom   Never
- Give at least a tithe and offerings to the church
  Always   Usually   Sometimes   Seldom   Never
- Provide leadership in the church
  Always   Usually   Sometimes   Seldom   Never

- Seek reconciliation with those I may have a problem with or who may have a problem with me
  Always   Usually   Sometimes   Seldom   Never
- Bless those within and outside the household of faith
  Always   Usually   Sometimes   Seldom   Never

"Witnessing for the Lord" (20-Point Maximum)

- Share your testimony with others
  Always   Usually   Sometimes   Seldom   Never
- Witness for Christ regularly to others outside your family-and-friends circle
  Always   Usually   Sometimes   Seldom   Never
- Share God's plan for salvation with others
  Always   Usually   Sometimes   Seldom   Never
- Follow up with those who have received Christ in church/community
  Always   Usually   Sometimes   Seldom   Never
- Encourage new converts in your local church
  Always   Usually   Sometimes   Seldom   Never

When you have finished, score your answers as follows:

Always = 4	Sometimes = 2	Never = 0
Usually = 3	Seldom = 1	

Total each category. Achieving the highest number of points possible within a category indicates that you have a strong discipleship walk in that area at the moment. Combine category totals to determine your overall score (132 points possible), which reflects a comprehensive look at your current level of discipleship.

STEPPING-STONES

The Three-Strand Cord

Devise your personal strategy for implementing the Three-Strand Cord.

1. Crowds—participate in large-group learning modules such as worship, Sunday school, or Bible study.

2. Classes—join a Circle of Friends that trains and encourages the participants to line up their thoughts, words, and deeds with the Word of God, bringing about a change in behavior.

3. Cells or core—join or start a group that focuses on character, conduct, and commitment to be a disciple of Jesus Christ, for yourselves or younger generations.

Live

*The thief comes only in order to steal and kill
and destroy. I came that they may have and enjoy
life, and have it in abundance [to the full, till it
overflows].*

JOHN 10:10 AMP

*Nourishing yourself in a way that helps you blossom
in the direction you want to go is...attainable, and
you are worth the effort.*

DEBORAH DAY

It's not until you almost die that you become more determined
to live, and this time try to do it up right," said one of Payne
Memorial's members. He'd been the picture of perfect physical
health until the day he got the devastating diagnosis: coronary
heart disease.

Andrew knew he should exercise more, and cut down on

the fatty and fried foods that are characteristic of our Western diet. He was a young man, not yet forty. In his mind, young men didn't have narrowing of the arteries because of the buildup of plaque. But in the prime of his life, Andrew's body forced him out of his bad habits.

Knowing what to do is different from actually doing it. Start small, then go big.

For twenty years, the United States Army recruited young men and women to join their ranks with a five-word challenge: "Be all you can be." With that single sentence, the army tapped into a basic human desire, especially within young people, to achieve something, to make an impact, and to explore the boundaries of their abilities.

Most of us desire to be all that we can be, whether we serve in the army or not. From birth until death, we have an invitation to accept the Creator's challenge to serve humanity with all of the gifts we have been given. Humorist Erma Bombeck once wrote: "When I stand before God at the end of my life, I would hope that I would not have a single bit of talent left and could say, 'I used everything you gave me.'" Some will transition from this life having used all they were divinely given. Others will die with many unused gifts inside of them.

There is possibly nothing more painful than to see a gifted person whose talent is wasted because they can't get it together. At some point in their lives, they lost the ability to make the choices that would keep them alive and healthy and capable of sharing their gifts with humanity.

We've mourned the loss of many great talents, only to discover that somewhere their lifestyle did not support a commitment to "live to live"—whether because of drug or alcohol abuse, excess weight and poor eating habits, hanging out in destructive and dangerous environments, or being victimized by someone else's destructive decision. But it's not just famous people who are sometimes guilty of not living to live. It happens to everyday people. The Centers for Disease Control has sponsored a series of public service announcements. One of them features a man named Brian, an air force veteran and a long-term smoker who developed heart disease. His career ended because, as he states, "It's hard to serve your country when you're too weak to put on a uniform."

It's hard for any of us to render service to God when we're not in good heath, and that includes more than physical health. We need to be in good health spiritually, mentally, relationally, and financially. To maintain the measure of health we have been given requires us to make the choices that support our choice to live to live. Those choices may include everything from losing weight to losing a destructive relationship.

The life choices we make play a critical role in determining both longevity and quality of life. A man who had struggled with numerous health problems lost over a hundred pounds and had begun to take his health seriously. A friend listened to all of the lifestyle adaptations the man had made and remarked, "Well, I'm going to eat what I want whenever I want. Something is going to kill me, anyway." The man replied, "That's true, but you may not die from eating whatever you want. You may just get sick enough to wish you were dead!"

How different would our lives be if, every day we awakened,

we made conscious choices to empower us to live our best life in every way? The decisions we make every day impact whether we can be strong physically, spiritually, mentally, emotionally, and financially. When we take care of our bodies, we are strong enough to be one of the laborers in God's plentiful harvest (see Matthew 9:37).

Nurturing our spiritual health keeps us connected to God and less vulnerable to being lured away from the things of God. Maintaining healthy relationships means we can live a stable lifestyle that allows us to focus our energies on using our gifts to serve humanity.

Another important form of health is in our finances. When we properly use the financial resources God has given us, we are less likely to have a lifetime of economic stress that distracts us from being all that God has created us to be.

Successful professional athletes who maintain long-term careers do not consistently engage in reckless behavior. We hear reports all the time of athletes arrested for some criminal action, but rarely are such athletes able to do both. It's hard to be a troublemaker and a well-trained, prepared athlete who is game ready. As Jesus said, we cannot serve God and mammon. We cannot be double-minded and expect to succeed (see Matthew 6:24).

You Are Always with You

"No matter where you go, there you are." The quote gives us something to think about. Although its origin is uncertain, the saying is quite popular in modern culture. It reminds us that we cannot escape ourselves. No matter what issues we may be dealing with from others, we can't escape ourselves. That's the most important reason to motivate us to live to live. In other words, choose behaviors and actions that sustain, enhance, and prolong life, rather than those that shorten life's quality or chronology.

If someone else irritates you, you can distance yourself from the person, even if only temporarily. You can never get away from yourself. And since there's no possible separation from self, we should strive to be our best selves.

It's a good feeling to find within you the best self that God created in you, and then to offer that self to God for service every day.

The Gospels contain numerous stories of Jesus healing people and restoring them to physical and emotional wholeness and into full participation in their community. At God's creation of the Garden of Eden, there was no sickness, and John envisioned a city in Revelation where death will be no more. Good health is the desire of God (see 3 John 1:2). Therefore, when we strive to be healthy and are instruments of good health and wholeness, we are doing the work of the Lord.

Trying to overhaul your eating patterns can be overwhelming. Establishing a pattern of regular exercise takes commitment. Faithful discipleship means taking action to attain or maintain the good health that God wants for all of us. Let the small changes to your eating patterns speak louder than your good intentions. Learn about your body: Get a book, go online, get regular doctor checkups, and talk to a professional about any pain or discomfort. And if you suffer a relapse, pick yourself up and start all over again.

Incorporating healthier eating habits with more physical activity can make a huge difference. Park farther away instead of circling the lot ten times for a closer space. Show your gratitude for the health and strength God has given you by using it! Love your body. Remember, it is the temple of the Holy Spirit. Treat it well and make sure everyone else does the same. When you honor your body, you honor the Lord.

Live *in* the Moment, Not *for* the Moment

A part of the challenge to live fully is being in the moment. We need to experience the transformation that allows us to be present at every moment. Living in the moment means not living in a bad past, or a good one either. All the things that happened to us before, positive and negative, and the ways we responded to those events, make us who we are today. Our past affects how we live, but continuing to ruminate over the past will not change our present. We have to learn what we need to learn from our experiences and then empty ourselves of those events. Give them to God so we can be healed and filled with God's Spirit.

Living in the moment also means not living for a good future. Many of us are planners, doers, and futurists. We set targets and goals and often overlook what we have in the present. Living in what has not yet happened means spending our energy hoping for something better to happen instead of finding enjoyment in the present today. We let tomorrow rob us of the precious here and now.

Living in the moment means not being consumed with worry over a possible bad future. How much time have you invested in worrying about a future outcome that never happened? Jesus tells us not to live in a bad future. "Can any one of you by worrying add a single hour to your life? So do not worry, saying, 'What shall we eat?' or 'What shall we drink?' or 'What shall we wear?' For the pagans run after all these things, and your heavenly Father knows that you need them. But seek first his kingdom and his righteousness, and all these things will be given to you as well" (Matt. 6:27, 31–33 NIV).

Living in the moment does not mean living *for* the moment. Living for the moment means we disregard the consequences of our actions for the pleasures and desires of the moment. We want what we want, and we want it now. We don't adopt the discipline of delayed gratification. Living for the moment is microwave living—instant everything.

Living for the moment is disregard for the future in favor of the present. That leads us to poor choices and dire consequences. It causes us to make bad priority decisions, to waste time and opportunities, to squander resources and assets.

Living for the moment is living without discipline or self-control. It avoids struggle or suffering—physical, mental, emotional—at whatever the cost. It is the attempt to bypass anything unpleasant, inconvenient, or uncomfortable.

Living for the moment is jumping every time your body whimpers. It is putting bandages on cancers to relieve the immediate pain. It is finding substitutes for real joy through alcohol, drugs, entertainment, food, pills, painkillers.

Living for the moment is a short-term, limited perspective. It rarely looks beyond today and seldom sees more than its own self. The moment has a small worldview, and self is at the center.

Jesus told a parable about a man who already had it good. His crop was good. Instead of enjoying the moment, he focused on building a bigger barn to hold even more. He was so excited thinking about what he was going to get, he totally forgot about what he already had. But God said to him, "You fool! This very night your life will be demanded from you. Then who will get what you have prepared for yourself?" Then Jesus said, "This is how it will be with anyone who stores up things for himself but is not rich toward God." (See Luke 12:16–21.)

We are called upon to live *in* the moment but not *for* the moment. Let's explore what it means to live in the moment.

Living in the moment recognizes the value of each instant as full of richness and magic. The passage of time, from one second to the next, is a miracle in its own right and worthy of savor. I am not advocating that we go through life ignoring the pain or the realities we face. Have the appropriate emotion for each moment. The time we are in right now is precious, because it will never come by again. We can only live right now and that is enough.

There's a saying: "If you pray, why worry? If you worry, why pray?" Now, worry is not the same as concern. Concern says, "This is an issue, and I will deal with it and get through it with God's help." Worry says, "I don't know what's going to happen. I don't know if I'll make it through."

Worry is one of the enemy's greatest weapons. It will steal your joy, steal your contentment, steal your happiness, and steal your common sense. We can become consumed by worry and miss opportunities that God has placed before us to impact people with our faith. Or we even risk having a negative effect on prospective believers because our worry exhibits a lack of faith.

When people of faith worry, we should stop to consider, "You know, I am presenting a picture here that I don't believe my God can handle this problem." In other words, would anyone want to know more about Jesus based on your life?

We can become so wrapped up in worry about tomorrow and resentment about yesterday that we never find peace today. Living this way hinders our ability to enjoy the abundant life Christ came to give us.

Believers need to be in a place of well-being so that we can share the hope of Christ with others, through both word and deed. Your faith walk is God's best appeal to a hopeless world. Therefore, how can you spread hope if you do not have it together, if you regard your own situation as hopeless? How can you inspire someone to have faith in God if you are worried and distraught? How can you spread joy if your face is always twisted up in anger, fear, or negativity?

Living in the moment means living in proper balance. We learn from the past, and that helps us to make the right choices for the moment, and we live preparing for the future, without it consuming our now.

God was introduced to Moses as "I Am," not "I Will Be," or "I Wish I Could Have Been," or "I Used to Be." That means God is about the right now of our lives, the present.

See God in Your Right Now

One of the Beatitudes tells us, "Blessed are the pure in heart, for they will see God" (Matt. 5:8 NIV). But if your heart is tainted by bitterness from the pain of the past or clogged with worry about the future, how can you see God?

When the Bible says you will see God, that also means you will see God in your present-day circumstances, not just in the afterlife. It is a promise to see the Spirit of the Lord moving in your life at this very moment, day by day. And when you clearly see the hand of God touching your life, you want to praise God for it.

You can be sitting at a six-figure job, wearing a fabulous St. John suit and Christian Louboutin shoes. But you still cannot see God because you're not living in your present circumstances.

Some people go to church every Sunday and they do not see God. You can have the most beautiful voice in the world and sing in the choir every Sunday and not see God. You can give more money in church than anyone else and not see God in your financial abundance.

You can be blessed with a good spouse, a beautiful home, a loving family, and a sharp mind, but still not see God in your circumstances.

When you live in the present you know God is working unseen in the background of your life. You can see God because even when the price of gasoline skyrockets, you trust God to stretch what you have so you are still able to fill your tank and get to work every day. You can see God in the fact that people are getting laid off all over your company, but by the favor of God you still have a job.

God is moving in our lives right now! If we open eyes of faith we can see God right now. God offers salvation right now! God has worked it out right now!

Temporal Matters Now

In the movie *The Color Purple*, Sofia (Oprah Winfrey) challenges Miss Celie (Whoopi Goldberg) about advising her stepson to beat Sofia in order to shift the balance of power in their marriage. Miss Celie rationalized that this life would soon be over, so just deal with things the way they are. The high-spirited Sofia gave Miss Celie a quick remedy for dealing with her here-and-now situation and stormed off!

Their disagreement was similar to a debate among the Corinthian believers about whether they needed to give attention to earthly matters since our ultimate home is heaven. Miss Celie was tolerating abuse under the belief that "there's a bright side somewhere," and only in heaven would she find relief from the abuse she had suffered since childhood.

The Corinthian Christians took the matter to a different level. They were freely engaging in sexual immorality, even though they were followers of Christ. They reasoned that since their fleshly bodies were only temporary, why be concerned about it? They could have sex with whomever they wanted and be as gluttonous as they wanted. What they did to their bodies didn't matter, because this life was temporary.

In the final verses of 1 Corinthians 6, Paul clarifies how believers should treat their bodies: "Your body is the temple of the Holy Spirit, who lives in you and was given to you by God[.] You do not belong to yourself, for God bought you with a high price. So you must honor God with your body" (vv. 19–20 NLT). Paul was specifically addressing sexual immorality, but we have a better quality of life when we honor God with our bodies in every way.

Sometimes our lives can get out of control. Our physical health can go awry. Our mental health can be put in jeopardy. Our spiritual soundness can be compromised. We can extend ourselves too far financially. Even if our lives are grossly imbalanced in one area or in many ways, the good news is we can begin again. As long as God gives us another day of life, we can begin to turn things around step-by-step.

Small Change Adds Up

That is the premise for Susan and Larry Terkel's book *Small Change: Little Things Make a Big Difference* (Tarcher/Penguin, 2004). The husband-and-wife team suggests that small changes are easier to initiate and maintain.

The authors also demonstrate how minimal changes, when sustained, can yield measurable results. For example, replace a soft drink with water at just one meal, like lunch. In one year you'll drink forty gallons of water instead of forty gallons of carbonated sugar. You'll lower your caloric intake by fifty thousand, and possibly add $500 to your wallet.

So often, when it comes to issues like weight loss, we want to make huge changes quickly. "I need to lose forty pounds before my class reunion next month!" Anyone who has attempted something like that will tell you that such resolutions rarely yield lasting results. You go on a crash diet and lose forty pounds. Then you resume your former eating pattern and gain back fifty pounds!

If you've done that, maybe it's time to consider some small changes that will help you reach your ultimate goal for better health. Our bodies adjust to small changes more easily than big, disruptive ones. You can't just get up off the couch and run a marathon.

Small changes require discipline, persistence, and vision. People often get discouraged and quit because what they desire seems to be taking too long. Paul encouraged the Galatian church, "Let us not become weary in doing good, for at the proper time we will reap a harvest if we do not give up" (Gal. 6:9 NIV).

You won't become a bodybuilder, or even complete a decent workout, if you cannot sustain the small changes. If your goal is not to become a fitness buff or if your weight is within acceptable levels, you can still take advantage of opportunities to increase your activity level and decrease your caloric intake.

Walk up a flight of steps or down two flights instead of waiting for the elevator. Park farther away from the building entrance. Do yard work or start a garden. Take your shopping cart back inside the store when you've unloaded your purchase. Walk to the next bus stop instead of just sitting at the closest one. All of this is small change that adds up.

Big doors swing on small hinges. Evolving into a lifestyle that empowers you to live to live means adopting manageable changes that do not disrupt everything in your life.

Small changes will not only help you feel better physically; better overall health also enhances your mental and emotional well-being. Scientific research consistently supports the connection between regular exercise and good mental and emotional health. Improved self-esteem has also been connected to regular physical activity.

As you exercise, your body releases chemicals known as endorphins and serotonin. These hormones interact with the receptors in your brain that reduce your perception of pain and increase mood enhancement. Recruit a friend to walk a few blocks with you two to three times a week. Increase it a few blocks at a time. Get up every ninety minutes from your desk and take a break.

In addition to physical exercise, you can incorporate a number of other smaller actions to improve your life and your relationships. Try saying, "I love you," at the end of a phone conversation with someone who's close to you. Let others know you appreciate having them in your life. Tell someone they did a good job on a project. Giving compliments and encouragement costs you nothing but reaps great benefits for you and for the recipient of your affirmations.

The same is true regarding difficult situations that may arise. Take a deep breath before reacting to annoyances. Save your angry e-mail as a draft for twenty-four hours before you hit Send. Pray before you speak to someone who opposes you. Go for a walk. Do the triple tithe: a tenth to the Lord, a tenth to savings, and a tenth for you.

You can try doing one fun thing for yourself a week or add at least an hour for friends or a hobby—small changes: Ask more and assume less; think before you speak; get enough sleep tonight; phone home; send a handwritten note instead of an e-mail to thank someone; eat popcorn instead of chips or nuts instead of cookies for snacks; switch to decaf anything; try three minutes of stretching in the morning, three minutes of prayer, three minutes of just being grateful, looking for things to be thankful about before beginning your regular routine, or just three minutes of praising God for who God is. It will make a difference in your day—one small change per month could add up to a big lifestyle change for you!

A small change eases you into new things. It doesn't require a massive amount of money, a drastic change of schedule, or a radical lifestyle change. It is a "one step at a time" promise of sustained success. And with one small success you'll work for more. Think of it as the steady progress of the tortoise that eventually wins the race instead of the rabbit.

It can all start by simply changing your mind. What small change can you make—today—that will make a big difference in your life later on?

Beware of Self-Sabotage

Try as you may in earnest to be your best self, be careful that you don't get in your own way. Moses was so close to the place promised by God. He had been effectively leading his mega congregation through the wilderness. He had established an administrative structure to help manage the people's concerns. At every turn, God protected and provided for them through many dangers, toils, and snares.

About a month after they arrived in the Desert of Zin, they ran out of water. The people panicked and grumbled to Moses that they were going to die. Moses sought the Lord's help, and God instructed him to speak to the rock and water would come out. In anger, Moses hit the rock twice instead. Maybe he was lashing out his frustrations on the stone. (See Numbers 20.)

Moses' actions shut him out of crossing into the Promised Land. He was on his way to leading his people from slavery in Egypt into the land God had assigned them, but his anger sabotaged the process.

Self-sabotage occurs when you say something, do something, or fail to do something and that takes the wind out of the sails of your dreams. As incongruent as it seems, many people sabotage their success. It can take many forms, like the promising corporate executive who gets caught doing insider trading. The pastor whose church is a beacon of light in the community is publicly exposed for unethical behavior. A young woman wins a full scholarship to a university, including room, board, and books, gets pregnant, and decides to marry and drop out of school.

Why do people circumvent their success? Maybe they feel they don't deserve the success—they secretly harbor feelings that they're not good enough, not ready, or somehow the moment is too good to last. It could be they're too familiar with failure; something always goes wrong. The perfectionist inside of them kicks them with thoughts that since it can't possibly work out, they might as well ditch it now to avoid embarrassment. Or they think, "Hmm, if this works out, my success might overshadow someone important to me," like a parent, a spouse, or a friend.

So what happens when you get an answer to what you've been praying for—a promotion, a new job, a new love, a house, or better circumstances? You reach the border of your promised land and suddenly you quit, walk away, or refuse to respond. You start to backpedal, show up late, don't do the work, won't make the final push, or you forget to fill out the forms or mail in your résumé. It was your idea, your baby. But on the launch day you were too stressed to have your ducks all in a row.

You've been waiting for that prime invitation that has the potential to open so many doors for you in the future. So you spend more time on your hair, nails, and wardrobe than on what you are supposed to do. The day arrives. You look good, but you go in all style and no substance.

People also engage in self-sabotage when they don't live to live. They don't take care of their health. They attach themselves to a string of unhealthy people and relationships. There are still too many leaders who maintain close connections with friends or family who want to engage in destructive behavior. The friends or family may have nothing to lose, but you could lose a job, a contract, or a good reputation because of what the people around you did.

Financial sabotage happens when people mishandle their finances, so they never get their credit straightened out. They rack up high amounts of credit card debt living above their income. They derail financial peace and prosperity because designer purses and shoes and luxury cars are more important than money in the bank. Their excess spending doesn't allow room for the money they should be using to tithe and invest in God's kingdom and in themselves and their future.

Physical sabotage means not maintaining health and appearance that are important to getting hired or to attracting a mate or to having the strength and agility needed to maintain a quality of life. Obesity is at epidemic levels in the United States. Related chronic health conditions are also on the rise—diabetes, heart disease, mobility issues, and the like.

Jesus cautions his disciples in John 10:10 that the world has thieves who wish to take from them to the point of destruction. By contrast, Jesus came to give life, one more abundant than anything previously known.

Jesus desires that we have an enjoyable life that yields good health in mind, body, and spirit. When we allow him to guide us through this greater form of living, we make choices that empower us to live to live.

Self-sabotage puts your attention on things that are not important by making them seem relevant to your life. Substance abuse is not necessary to living well. Destructive relationships are not necessary for a good life. Financial instability is not an ingredient of life's best recipe. Toxic spirituality and emotional volatility do not contribute to abundant living. These are detrimental to a person determined to live to live.

Lay Aside Every Weight

The word *aerodynamic* comes from two Greek words: *aerios*, concerning the air; and *dynamikos*, meaning "powerful." So aerodynamics is the study of forces and the resulting motion of objects through the air. All modern modes of transportation— planes, trains, and automobiles—are designed to be aerodynamic. They are crafted to reduce wind drag and thereby increase their speed and fuel efficiency.

Christians should be the same way in our Christian walk. We should discipline and shape ourselves to reduce the likelihood of people or circumstances dragging us down. Hebrews 12:1 cautions us to "lay aside every weight, and the sin which doth so easily beset us" (KJV).

Christians who are training themselves to live to live have to get rid of excess weight. Imagine Serena Williams trying to run up and down the tennis court carrying an extra fifty pounds. She can't win if she's encumbered by unnecessary weight. In order to be competitive, she wears gear that is very formfitting so that it won't slow her down or hinder her in any way. Every impediment to speed is laid aside. She must be aerodynamic when she plays.

The weights that amount to self-sabotage are different for each of us. For some, it's the telephone. There's nothing wrong with talking on the telephone, but when God wants you focused on something else, the phone becomes a weight because it impedes progress. Too much time spent on social media can weigh you down. Competitiveness can cause people to circumvent their own success because they're consumed by keeping up with the Joneses. Envy, jealousy, anger, and pettiness are all weights some of us may have to lay aside. Others may have to lay aside some friends. The friends may not be bad people, and they may even be Christians, but the problem is that they're excess weight. For some, the past or a preoccupation with what people are saying about them may need to be laid aside, or another bad habit. Whatever it is, only by laying that weight down can we be successful in drawing closer to God.

STEPPING-STONES

Create a list of ten small changes you can make that will have long-term benefits to your mental, physical, spiritual, financial, and overall well-being. If your finances are in sound shape, concentrate on improving your physical, spiritual, or emotional strength.

1. Phase One: Make three columns. In the first column, write down the category where you believe personal improvement is needed in your life (Physical, Mental, Spiritual, Financial). In the second column, write down small changes you can make, like parking farther away from every building entrance, especially at places like the movies, the grocery store, and so forth. Cut down on your carbohydrates by eliminating bread from one meal a day or refusing dessert except on the weekends or when you're eating out. To improve your financial strength, look at paying off one credit card at a time, the smallest balance first. Start making your own coffee at home instead of indulging in that expensive cup you drink every morning. Start doing your own nails. Practice saying "Thank you" and complimenting people when they do a good job. It will improve your mental and emotional strength. In the third column, put a timeline

for when you hope to see noticeable improvement in this area.

2. Phase Two: Look at all the areas from Phase One and pump up the volume! Consider how you can improve on the incremental changes you already have made.

3. Continue to add a new phase of life with tweaks when you sense it is time to take your small changes to the next level.

Be Church

Now you are the body of Christ, and each one of you is a part of it.

1 Corinthians 12:27 NIV

Christians often want to hide behind the walls of the church, where we are comfortable, but sometimes we have to come out of the box.

Cheryl "Salt" James (Salt-N-Pepa)

He's churched, not changed!" Floretta complained about her husband. "He's been going there for most of his adult life, but he's still living the same. He goes in one way and comes out the same way."

"Getting inside the church is one thing. Letting Christ get inside your lifestyle is another," I responded. "We must be the church, not just in the church." Old things pass off the scene and a new life emerges (see 2 Corinthians 5:17).

You may have said many times, "I'm going to church on

Sunday," without giving it much thought. But that statement would have confused members of the early church, because they did not regard church as a building or location. They *were* the church! In all they said and did, they were the Body of Christ. Church was not a place from which they could depart. Church was not a place to go; it was a way of living.

You are the church, which is why worship happens even when you are far away from sanctuary in a house of worship. It's the reason why you can feel God even if you haven't been to church in years.

All of our readings in the Gospels and the New Testament are instructions for teaching us how to be the church. We're it. We are all Christ has to carry out his mission. And the amazing thing is: As flawed, insecure, and inconsistent as human beings can be, God still manages to get meaningful service from us. Even believers who have been in church for years and years sometimes think of others as being more righteous and more worthy to do the Lord's work. Yet a survey of the Bible quickly enumerates a roll call of imperfect men and women whom God used to make a difference.

God's Spirit has given us gifts, so that we may make a difference as the church, to support and encourage one another as sisters and brothers in Christ. Later in 1 Corinthians 12, Paul compares the Body of Christ to a human body, where no one part is more important than the other.

Looking at the entirety of chapter 12, we glimpse God's design for the Body of Christ. We have diversity, and we have gifts to encourage and support one another. It's up to us whether we use our gifts and diversity to support the Body of Christ and expand the kingdom of God. Or we can use our gifts and diversity to fuel competitiveness and division. Paul says its God's job to decide the role each part should play. "But our bodies have many parts, and God has put each part just where he wants it. How strange a body would be if it had only one part! Yes, there are many parts, but only one body. The eye can never say to the hand, 'I don't need you.' The head can't say to the feet, 'I don't need you'" (1 Cor. 12:18–21 NLT).

Each of us matters in the Body of Christ because we are all the church. How does your understanding of church change when your own face is an essential part of it? That means the church cannot be at its best if you are not serving, according to your gifts. The church cannot do all that it was designed to if you are not making yourself available.

Since all believers make up the church, each of us must discern the way we function individually within the Body of Christ, according to the gifts we are given. If you are not aware of how God has gifted you, start praying about how your gifts may be revealed to you. Your gifts may be such a part of your behaviors that you never even consider them to be something special. Think about the thing that people are always asking you to do.

"Go Ye Therefore…"

In his Great Commission, Jesus extends an invitation to his disciples to go into the world and be the church (see Matthew

28:19–20). Each of us operates as the church when we follow Jesus' method of drawing in believers.

People were drawn to Jesus because he had the power to help and to heal. He helped people without judgment or condemnation, like Zacchaeus the tax collector (see Luke 19:1–10), blind Bartimaeus, Mary Magdalene, and the unnamed woman caught in adultery (see John 8:1–11). We, too, have the power to draw people to Christ. Fortunately, this power does not depend on our individual personalities. Our magnetic power lies within our faith as the main draw.

But if all of the world's distractions are gripping people's attention, how can God's people compete? Just as the Samaritan woman at the well was looking for satisfaction in her relationships with men, Jesus told her, "Whoever drinks the water I give will never thirst."

When people come to Christ, they find satisfaction. That is why Christ emphasizes that it is he who must be lifted up. Jesus did not say "if the church be lifted up," or "if our theology be lifted up," or "if our traditions are lifted up." Christ alone has the power to draw people away from all the world has to offer.

We can guide people to find satisfaction in Christ by sharing our own stories of repentance. Think back to who you were when you began your walk with Christ in earnest. Have you, through Christ, experienced a metamorphosis? Does the person you are today resemble the person you were then? Hopefully, as you have walked in the way of Christ, you have experienced the repentance Jesus began to preach in Matthew 4:17.

Repentance, as conveyed in the New Testament, is expressed in three Greek words, each starting with the syllable *meta*. It is the root of the word *metamorphosis*, indicating a change or a renewal. Just as a caterpillar's development into a butterfly is a metamorphosis, our journey in Christ brings change that is beyond recognition of what was.

That's how we live church. Instead of sitting uprightly on our favorite church pew on Sunday morning, conducting ourselves as if we've behaved in a saved and sanctified manner every day of our lives, we each can tell people how, through Christ, "I ain't what I used to be!"

We live church when we are willing to talk about what happens when the power of Jesus Christ enters people's lives. People love to hear a success story. We can live our success story and we can share the victories that come through life in Christ, rather than meting out judgment and unforgiveness and withholding mercy and grace.

You have a choice to live as a church member, a disciple of Jesus Christ, while you are within the doors of the church building, associating with those who look, act, and believe as you do. Or you can live as the church, completely, day by day, taking the message of good news to all who would hear it. Your spirit can be attuned to the needs of those around you as you demonstrate God's love through meeting the needs of the "least of these" (Matt. 25:40 NLT).

Church at Its Best

What does the church look like at its best? The church at its best is a living organism that operates under a banner of "No longer business as usual."

Everything that Jesus said during his earthly ministry—what he did, and how he did it—instituted change. His presence challenged the old way of doing and thinking, no matter how beloved or treasured the former things were. Every miracle he performed brought change over forces and systems that theretofore had represented the definitive answer regarding human and institutional predicaments.

The church at its best invades the norm and creates a new normal, according to the dictates of the kingdom, not the whims of culture. It colors outside the lines of the politically correct to work with God in whatever God is doing and not to be just busy.

The church at its best is the messenger of prophecy, where there is *chazown*, a Hebrew word that means "a fresh revelation." It is God's knowledge revealed by the Holy Spirit that will keep you so that you are not overwhelmed by the darkness or so caught up in it that you lose your way among the people, places, and things that constantly demand your attention.

The church at its best is not merely a repository of programs. The "every third Sunday, first Saturday after the fourth, right after homecoming, between men's and women's days, every member's birthday, and turn in your envelope" church; the "food and fellowship only" church; the "follow the program as printed" church; the "well-designed programmatic structure around membership program, seeker program, education program, outreach program, worship program, evangelism program" church. The light of revelation flickers among the programs, and those who were once people of destiny now are demoralized. They then become disobedient to the faith and to God's Word.

The church at its best is impressed with God rather than with itself. It focuses on the things of God—worship in spirit and in truth. The church that knows the truth will not be misled by opinion or the lesser things of culture and society.

The church at its best rises to become a viable force with which to contend, no matter its size, location, structure, or substance. It refuses to be a run-of-the-mill box on a denominational chart. A run-of-the-mill church is predictable. You know what's going to be said. You know what everyone is going to do. You know where everyone sits and stands. It molds for itself a programmatic rut, doing the same things over and over. Maybe change the names once in a while, but if it's not in the *Discipline*, the calendar, or the bulletin, it can't be done.

Sometimes we need to be reminded that the church at its best is the "whatever it takes" church. It's the Body of Christ open to new leadings of the Holy Spirit and to possibilities for the future. The people who are the church don't settle for good enough, but rather, they keep asking, "Is better possible?"

They choose to be proactive rather than protect the status quo. They're constantly reaching out to and for other people; the church is forgiven, reaching out to the good, the bad, and the ugly.

Sometimes we need to be reminded that the church at its best lives at the end of its comfort zone—never satisfied with where they are or with the cards they've been dealt. They constantly stand up to circumstances that seem unchangeable and the problems that won't disappear. They are not afraid of the possibilities of the future. This body of believers doesn't look back long, but plays and pays it forward, constantly seeking God's vision rather than satisfying its own interest.

Being the Church Ain't Easy!

Mark 2 begins the narratives detailing reports of conflict between Jesus and the religious authorities. There is always conflict when there are drastic differences of opinion. Those who *thought* they knew who Jesus was came into direct conflict with who Jesus *really* was. A new reality had emerged and was being played out in front of them.

When God begins to shift business as usual into a new reality, there will always be conflict between what was and what is going to be. Conflict between what people think they know and what really is; conflict between natural and supernatural, the invisible and the visible, and between the movement of God and the pace of congregational culture.

Mark 2:1–2 tells us that Jesus' message had gone viral. It was as if he had millions of Twitter followers and Facebook friends. Great crowds came to see him in the arenas of every town he visited.

A crowd showed up to hear Jesus speak. The house was filled to capacity, so full that there was no room in front of the doorways or windows. A group of concerned citizens started a selfless new initiative outside the walls of the house. They focused on one whom they believed was greater than the people knew at that moment.

The four men who initiated the movement were able to look beyond the obvious problem and pain of a man incapacitated on his pallet of affliction. Together they picked him up and carried him to the house where Jesus was preaching. The people inside were engaged in worship, oblivious to what was happening on the outside. Sometimes we're so busy having church, we forget to be the church and help those who have been left on the outside.

Everybody showed up to hear the preaching, enjoying their position in the room. "I got my seat; you get yours."

Thank God there were four men who were more interested in being the church than being in church. They put forth an extraordinary effort to give an outsider access to Jesus. They had to believe that whatever the paralytic was going through, Jesus could fix it. The man was more than the sum total of his problem or pain.

Praise God for the church that can see beyond problems and pain and can look beyond our wretched condition to focus on our potential and believe in a better day and a better life for us. They see the best in us and are not afraid of it, and they won't try to destroy it, control it, clone it, or deny it. They are not swayed by our mistakes and see the good in us that we haven't even seen in ourselves.

They saw something in this man who had been unable to function as a decision-making, productive member of the community, a drain on the budget who may have already had one or more rescue efforts. He couldn't do what was necessary to change his own plight, but four men decided to be the church and change the trajectory of his life. They refused to accept the majority report and took action and responded. This is the church at its best.

The people were a barrier. The building was a barrier. The load they were carrying was a barrier. God doesn't move the barriers in front of us but will give us power to handle them and the strength to push forward and move beyond them.

Being the church means serving God as much outside as worshipping on the inside. The paralytic was healed, but it wasn't because of a church program. It was the people being the church outside of its walls. The miracle that happened wasn't a dictate of the steward board or a project of the trustees. There was no church conference, official board, or quarterly conference, just four people who saw a problem and worked together because they had the faith to believe that their intervention would make a difference.

Being the church means being unafraid to try new approaches to ministry. They tried the door, but the door didn't work. They tried the window, but that plan was no good, either. They were determined to get to Jesus, so they broke through the roof to get to him.

Ours is no longer the world of "What do we do to make them come?" Now it's "What do we do to go get them and bring them in?" The four men refused to give up until their disenfranchised brother was made whole and brought into the fold.

The church at its best never gives up on trying to get people to the Lord! They pushed beyond the natural barriers of their time—people, building, and a structure that kept folks out. They were trying to get someone in, and we must do the same.

Leave It All in the Kingdom

In sports, athletes say, "Leave it all on the field," to indicate their intention to give their all to the game and hold nothing back. The game should always end with the athlete feeling "I gave it my all." When you live in continual awareness that you are the church, you are giving Christ your all. Your charge is to "leave it all in the kingdom," so that you don't live feeling as if you could do more.

In the movie *Schindler's List,* an emotional moment occurs near the end when businessman Oskar Schindler realizes he could have saved even more Jews from extermination. He looks at his possessions and considers how the money used to purchase those things could have saved people. Schindler did a lot, saving an estimated twelve hundred Jews from the gas chambers, but in his heart he knew more could have been done. Today an estimated seven thousand people are descendants of those he saved. But as World War II neared the end, Schindler could not rejoice in his own daring, because he wished he had done more.

Maybe you could be doing more to help secure housing for homeless people. Perhaps you could be giving more service to stop human trafficking. You could be tithing or giving more in offerings to support church ministries and programs. You could be giving more of your gifts to expand the kingdom rather than to increase your personal fortune.

Strive to offer God more than "doing just enough to get by" discipleship when you have the gifts and the opportunity to do something greater. Have you ever left a concert feeling like the performer didn't give his or her all? Would you ever want that to be said about your Christian service?

The Christian journey is a long-distance race, and we're all bound to have some periods when we are not at our best. But over a lifetime of service, the goal for every believer should be to give all to Christ, holding nothing back. Even when we aren't totally certain we are on the right path, we always should give our all.

Go with the Flow

The kingdom of God is like a river, an untamed surge of energy that can change a life and a landscape, writes author and church planter Neil Cole (*Church 3.0*, Jossey-Bass, 2010).

The kingdom of God is not static. It is not staid, but rather it is a movement. God's kingdom has a flow, a direction where its energy moves. It cannot go in two directions at the same time; one current of the river will submit to the other, even rough white water. When the water settles, the two currents will have merged into the flow, assert Chip and Dan Heath, coauthors of *Made to Stick: Why Some Ideas Survive and Others Die* (Random House, 2007).

And we, the disciples of Jesus Christ, are called to join the flow of the kingdom's river; not just to add it to our to-do list, but to cut through rough ground and bring living water to the thirsty. Our mission reminds me of a children's song:

I've got a river of life flowing out of me
Makes the lame to walk, and the blind to see.
Opens prison doors, sets the captives free
I've got a river of life flowing out of me.

Through the prophet Isaiah's eyes we are told that God would establish a river in an unlikely place (see Isaiah 43:18–19). There had never been any water on that dry pinnacle where the temple was located. Jerusalem had no natural river or water supply. The River is Jesus, who will come to the temple on the last feast day and declare that anyone who thirsts should come drink from him and never thirst again (see John 7:37). This River is mentioned in the Revelation of John, who saw a New Jerusalem.

The power of Isaiah's vision is that the River trickled and

then flowed mightily into the land beyond the temple. The River is not a creation of human effort. It comes from God, and both people and land will be blessed by God's gift of transformation beyond human expectation.

A new life and a new future come from the River.

The River will widen your circle of concern and deepen your faith. The River goes beyond former boundaries and previous limitations to a fresh interpretation of the future. This living, moving water is not destroying traditions but rather reinterpreting them for newer generations. The River doesn't limit what is or what used to be, but defines new areas of operation.

The River in Ezekiel's vision went through the wilderness and changed it. Trees grew where there were none. Fruit grew. Plants thrived. Lush green replaced parched land. Fish spawned and the land produced. What once had been throwaway land turned productive. An area that was ignored now became important, because the river went through the wilderness and changed the lay of the land. Its freshwater neutralized the Dead Sea.

That is why the church must be the River as well as the reservoir. The church must widen its circle of concern and be the transformer of lives and communities. The River will widen your vision and your circle of concern to include the wilderness and become an ever-deepening experience of the eternal and its manifestation in the world.

People have often asked me what it's like to be a bishop.

The reality of the episcopacy came to me while I was riding in the back of a pickup truck, going around the edge of a mountain on a tiny rough road to visit a congregation that had not seen a bishop in over one hundred years. It came as I was feeding and holding AIDS-stricken babies, putting them to sleep because their mothers were too ill to do so. The reality was helping missionaries sweep out the house of the patriarch of African Methodism in Botswana as he lay on his deathbed at the age of 104. It was high up in the Maloti Mountains, where I helped to start a brick-making business so that pastors could expand their churches and the community could build homes out of stone rather than reeds. It became real as I was serving in places that couldn't bless me back.

I challenge you to make wherever you are better and leave a firm foundation for the next generation to build upon, for every round goes higher and higher. Let the flow of the River guide you to places of service that you never knew existed.

Live Church for the Next Generation

Israel's entrance into the Promised Land was an event that God wanted firmly etched in Hebrew history. Therefore, God gave them instructions for inspiring curiosity about Israel's journey from slavery to the land God had established for them (see Joshua 4:21).

God has given parents primary responsibility for passing on

their faith to their children. But the entire body of faith has an important role in teaching young people how to live faith.

When your children become young adults and they face difficult situations, the legacy of faith they've received will enable them to make it through those times. Human beings can remember only what they see and experience, so your children won't remember to pray if they didn't see you praying. They won't remember to forgive if you never forgave anyone. They won't remember to praise God if they never saw you giving praise.

Wise parents model faithful living for their children during their developmental years. Parents can't afford to wait until the world has conditioned young people to be everything but faithful and then try to tell them, "Oh, by the way, I need to tell you what faith can do."

Parents teach their children about faith and action. God has given this responsibility to parents, not to the church. The church is not a babysitter. Children's choirs and youth ministries are not babysitters. Parents have a responsibility to be the church, not simply send their children to church.

Children need to see their parents worship God, both inside the church and outside its walls, because they won't remember it if they don't see it for themselves. As children grow up, parents should be telling them bedtime stories about David and how he fought Goliath, because when they are grown up, they are going to face some giant. They can't know they can defeat Goliath if no one ever told them they could.

Parents live church by precept and example and demonstrate for children how they can survive in the heat of troubling times. When children know that God will make a way, they won't need to run to a bottle of pills or alcohol to drown their sorrows.

What better tribute to good parenting than to hear an adult recall how their parents lived church. "I remember what Momma always told me about the importance of prayer," or, "My daddy taught me to turn to the Lord when the odds are stacked against you."

That's hard for some parents, because they are timid and insecure about witnessing to their children, so they pay the preacher to witness to their children. But no preacher can do what God wants and expects parents to do. Parents are supposed to live church and train their children in the way they should go.

Parents must teach their children, just like the father taught the prodigal son and his brother. He had to have taught them all along, but he also taught them as young adult men. He taught the prodigal son and his brother a valuable lesson in forgiveness and acceptance. The prodigal son knew to go to his father. Our children need to know that they can go to the Lord, who is always ready to receive them with rejoicing.

Tell your children how nobody got sick even when you lost your job and your health benefits. That way, when they get older, they'll remember who to turn to when life gets rough.

God wants you to tell the story of what God has done for you. Tell it to your children and future generations. Tell it to remind yourself. Tell of the victories that God has brought you through so the next generation will praise God for deliverance, too.

Explain that God showed you how to trust God enough to tithe. Reveal how God provided after you lost your job and pulled you through sickness. Share how God protected you when others tried to set you up. Let them know how God has guided you to right places, time after time.

God wants us to remember the past because God uses the past as a foundation for the future. There's a continuum of divine activity that we should be aware of. In other words, what God has done throughout the course of history, God will do again.

Many have gone before us, and many will follow. God wants us to value the past and respect it. God wants us to remember the journey and how we made it over. Those stories are not reserved just for Sunday or Wednesday night. Our testimonies are made known while we live church.

Future generations need to know that every single time God was right there at your bedside, in your car seat, in your work cubicle, in your kitchen, or in your bathroom. Wherever it seemed circumstances were about to overtake you, God acted right before your eyes and kept you and your family safe.

Our children must know the saving power of Jesus Christ, and they will know it only from us.

A great sea of youthful faces watches how we live. Therefore, it's naïve to say, "This is my life. And it's nobody's business how I live it." You cannot then say to your children, "Do as I say and not as I do." The Bible says that no one lives solely for him- or herself (see Romans 14:7). The arenas of our lives are filled with spectators. Young people are watching you to learn how to navigate through life.

God not only told parents to teach their children God's ways, but God instructed them to do it diligently. God said to do it throughout the day when the children are sitting, walking, going to bed, or getting up in the morning.

We have to pass the faith baton. In the 1948 Olympics, the entire US relay team was disqualified because one team member failed to pass his baton. The previous runners had run well. The runners who were waiting never got to run because one runner did not pass the baton.

Someone passed the baton to you, giving you a legacy of faith. Who is waiting on you to pass the faith along? Will you be there to pass or will you drop the baton?

Get in the Church and Be the Church

God has designed us to worship in fellowship with other believers. From the Old Testament to the New Testament, God's people have served side by side to carry out their marching orders.

More members in a local church means more voices giving praise to God, more people to give to the ministries that serve God's purposes, and more hands and feet to do the work of God. More members means more spiritual gifts at work in the kingdom and within the congregation. More members means more economic resources for ministry development and expansion.

People are always eager to join a movement, but not a ministry—not even a meaningful one. If you have not joined a church, find one that fits you and join. If you have joined but are not active, go back and connect with a ministry that will make room for your gifts to be groomed and grow.

If you are already involved in church, think about whether you are engaged in ministry that fulfills you and makes full use of your gifts. Or are you simply doing what you've always done? If you have been serving as an usher for twenty years and your service has become perfunctory, perhaps your calling is to serve through the diaconate or outreach ministries. The time and talent you give back to God should be meaningful to you.

Align yourself with ministries about which you can be passionate because you feel they are purposeful and penetrating. Be excited and determined to fulfill your calling. Be more than a church spectator. Go all in for Jesus!

Become both a stakeholder and a shareholder in the ministry of your church so that you can be a part of the movement that reaches beyond the church's walls to impact communities.

STEPPING-STONES

1. Create your "I Think the Church Ought to Be Doing" list. Come up with five or six ideas that are doable, given the resources of your church or a local church where you would like to do service or be the church. Prayerfully consider pulling together people who can help you implement the ministry. In the process, you may find a church that's already involved in a ministry where you would like to join in.

2. Schedule an appointment with your pastor or with the pastor of a local church you've considered joining. Find out what their ministries are and where you can fit in. Discuss the ministries on your list and the feasibility of implementing them at the church.

3. Make a list of ways you can be the church when you're outside church walls.

4. Determine to what extent you are able to be the church through intentional acts of love, grace, mercy, and redemption. Your actions may include anything from making a financial contribution to a long-term commitment of volunteer service. Don't be afraid to think beyond traditional ministry opportunities. Be

as bold and radical as Jesus was as he ministered to people who needed love and forgiveness.

5. Create a personal calendar with concrete actions and deeds you can do to be the church in your home, in your community, in your workplace, or among friends. Commit to one deed each week, and then increase your ministry efforts as you go.

Serve God with Intention

Do not be conformed to this world, but be trans-
formed by the renewal of your mind, that by testing
you may discern what is the will of God, what is
good and acceptable and perfect.

ROMANS 12:2 ESV

Jesus Christ died to save us from our sins; we tend
to concentrate on that merciful fact. But isn't it also
true He lived to show us a lifestyle free from sin? So,
wouldn't following in His footsteps be something like
preventative medicine?

RICHELLE E. GOODRICH

I treasure the peace I found that Sunday while sitting in the last row of my very first congregation, the peace that said, "God is in charge." I could go to sleep on that every night. I still treasure what I heard in my heart from God: "You're looking for ways to grow the people. I'm looking to grow you."

Before you begin to help someone else, you first must invest in your own growth and development. Whether you are launching a maiden voyage of discipleship with intention and focus or you endeavor to take your followship to a higher level, never forget that *self-care* is not a profane word.

Changing the big picture of your faith through small steps to grow closer to God and lead a deeper life of discipleship doesn't happen instantaneously. The journey of growing in grace and faith in Christ is lifelong, with twists, sharp turns, detours, and parking lots. There will be times when you feel like you're going backward rather than forward, like I did when four of my seven members died at my first pastoral assignment.

Anyone with any sense at all would want to live without trouble in his or her life. If we could, we'd all live without disappointments, failure, mistakes, regrets, crises, and sorrow.

If we could arrange it, friends would always be friendly, lovers would always be attentive, spouses would always be considerate, parents would always understand, and children would always make us proud.

If we could make it so, temptation would never call our name, sin wouldn't know us, and Satan could never catch us. We would want perfect churches, flawless pastors, stellar ministries, loving members, faultless disciples, impeccable Bible studies, and unparalleled singing.

That's the world we would wish for. But the one we actually live in is a different story. Upsets occur, disappointment knocks, problems invade, Satan returns, and into each life some rain must fall. The Bible cautions that in this life we shall have tribulation. James 1:2–4 says, "Dear brothers and sisters, when troubles of any kind come your way, consider it an opportunity for great joy. For you know that when your faith is tested, your endurance has a chance to grow. So let it grow, for when your endurance is fully developed, you will be perfect and complete, needing nothing" (NLT).

Paul writes to the believers in Philippi to thank the church for sending gifts after they learned he had been confined in Rome. He also used the occasion to encourage a vigorous style of Christian living: Be humble, press toward the goal of the high calling in Jesus Christ, release anxiety and empowerment to do all things in Christ Jesus. (See Philippians 3:1–10.)

In the letter, Paul tells us where to find the power to handle life's ups and downs, ins and outs, twists and sharp turns, around and through challenges. He shares that the most important thing in life is knowing Christ and experiencing the power of his resurrection (see v. 10). Our relationship to Christ gives us power to be better and overcome life's trials. It is a power that helps us see problems as opportunities, breakups as breakthroughs, and roadblocks as invitations for innovative solutions.

The word *power* occurs fifty-seven times in the New Testament. It is used to describe the most powerful event that made humankind change from BCE to CE. Jesus' resurrection from the grave gives us resurrection power to handle our lives during troubling times and to change our lives forever.

To the church at Ephesus, Paul writes, "I also pray that you will understand the incredible greatness of God's power for us who believe him. This is the same mighty power that raised Christ from the dead and seated him in the place of honor at God's right hand in the heavenly realms" (Eph. 1:19–20 NLT).

Paul uses the Greek word for "power"—*dunamis*—from which we get the English word *dynamite*. God gives us dynamite power that can change our lives. The same power that raised Jesus from the grave can transform our weaknesses into strengths.

Resurrection power is the might we need to cancel our past. God's sovereign authority will cancel our past. Yesterday is dead and gone; it slipped away while you slept. Therefore, you cannot alter it, relive it, or improve it. The hands of the clock will not go backward.

It's hard to take full advantage of the day God gives you when your life is caught up in yesterday. So, if you messed up yesterday, said the wrong thing, took a wrong turn, loved the wrong person, took the wrong job, or spent more than you should have, walked when you should have run, talked when you should have listened, trusted when you should have investigated, or indulged when you should have resisted, don't allow what happened yesterday to sabotage your day of opportunity. God's mercies are new every morning. Receive them and become drenched in God's grace. God has forgiven you, now you forgive yourself!

God's power will help us change our lives and impact others. When we accept Christ as Lord and Savior and endeavor to be an intentional disciple, we discover there is power available to us beyond our human flesh: Greater is he who dwells within us than he that is in the world (see 1 John 4:4).

When we allow God's power to stand up in us, the mess turns into a message of victory. The problem turns into possibilities. When you let God's power stand up in you, the mess turns into miracles, mistakes into merriment; problems become potential and crises turn into conquests, trials into triumphs, and tragedy into testimonies. So stand in anticipation that God is going to do great and marvelous things, in you, with you, through you, and for you!

The Bible gives us so many examples of people whose lives were changed in powerful ways because of their intentional pursuit of God's will and God's ways. One New Testament believer stands out because of his relentless determination to get close to Jesus. Every disciple is called to pursue Jesus, despite obstacles, criticisms, and discouragement.

It was festival time in Jerusalem, and Passover—the most solemn and sacred of all Jewish holidays—was being observed in the capital city of Jerusalem. All roads led to Jerusalem. The Jericho Road was the interstate of the ancient world, and as the Messiah was passing through, there was a flurry of activity there. So strategic was this travel route that it is still being used today.

Instead of moving down the road amid the throng of activity, Bartimaeus sat along the roadside while the parade passed him by. He sat while others traveled along singing, because his was a life of perpetual darkness. Blindness was even more crippling during ancient times—there were no Seeing Eye dogs; there was no Braille for him to decipher messages or psalms; nor were there any other amenities to assist those who were visually challenged. Exacerbating as blind Bartimaeus's circumstances were, he also was broke. The only economic avenue open to him was begging and panhandling.

What really had Bartimaeus sidelined was not simply blindness; it was a burdened heart. He had become a victim of his circumstances. He was beaten down by his inner stance, the kind that tells you things will never change; there are no new roads, only dead ends, ahead.

Bartimaeus made a small step that was a big deal, and it changed the trajectory of his life and his relationship with God. He made a decision to get closer to Jesus.

Initiative is the act of taking the first step or assuming responsibility for your predicament. Bartimaeus's life changed when he decided nothing would stop him from getting closer to Jesus. It was time for a change in Bartimaeus's life.

Maybe you've determined that it's time for you to get closer to Jesus and you're ready to at least take a small step forward. It's time for you to take some deliberate steps that will position you closer to the life-changing, life-enhancing power of Jesus Christ.

There's a saying familiar to 12-step programs: "If nothing changes, nothing changes." In order for conditions to change and for you to grow to intentionally lead a deeper life of faith, you must take the initiative to change. Jesus is always there. He's always waiting on you to take steps to get closer to him.

A lot of Christians sit on their faith as they watch others travel the road to being better. They experience spiritual growth in a random fashion. They wonder why they are on the sidelines rather than moving with the happy, enthused people who are moving along the road. They may envy someone who seems to have achieved what they want for themselves.

Bartimaeus wanted to be whole. He wanted to travel on the active road where people were enjoying life, so he determined to make a bold step, and no one and nothing was going to hinder him.

Have you watched as someone else seems to fulfill their life goals, realize their dreams, or utilize their energy to focus on the things of God? You've seen them rebound from circumstances that should have buried them in depression. You've watched them navigate challenges empowered by the gospel transformed by the Holy Spirit. You've seen them shed negative behaviors and habits by intentionally living out the fruit of the Spirit. They were riddled in shame; now they are "leading a new life following the commandments of God, walking henceforth in holy ways" (AME Communion liturgy: The Bidding).

Taking initiative always begins with your thought life. William James, known as the father of American psychology, said you can change your life by changing your attitude. Before the emergence of the science of psychology, the Bible said, "As he thinketh in his heart, so is he" (Prov. 23:7 KJV). "Do not conform to the pattern of this world, but be transformed by the renewing of your mind. Then you will be able to test and approve what God's will is—his good, pleasing and perfect will" (Rom. 12:2 NIV).

The Message version of the Bible says it this way: "So here's what I want you to do, God helping you: Take your everyday, ordinary life—your sleeping, eating, going-to-work, and walking-around life—and place it before God as an offering. Embracing what God does for you is the best thing you can do for him. Don't become so well-adjusted to your culture that you fit into it without even thinking. Instead, fix your attention on God. You'll be changed from the inside out. Readily recognize what he wants from you, and quickly respond to it. Unlike the culture around you, always dragging you down to its level of immaturity, God brings the best out of you, develops well-formed maturity in you" (Rom. 12:1–2).

A Mind to Be Better

Cultivating the right attitude for God to bring out the best in you and reach new levels of spiritual maturity is not about your education, your past, your looks, or your finances. It's all about attitude. You can direct your attitude and determine that you are going to do whatever it takes to be changed and be better, like blind Bartimaeus.

Bartimaeus wanted a better life. He knew that Christ had the power to help him achieve his goal to lead a new life. After he heard that Jesus was in the crowd, Bartimaeus had a change of attitude. He decided he was no longer a victim or a beggar to be pitied. That day, Bartimaeus became a man determined to get close to Jesus.

Some of us are just an attitude away from a breakthrough or a blessing. Take the challenge to adopt the intentional practices of this book so you can lead a new life—greater in grace and deeper in faith, following the Word and will of Jesus Christ. When you follow Christ on purpose, you can live in certain circumstances, but your circumstances don't have to live in you. Your present does not have to determine or define your ability to move into your future. It doesn't matter where you start, it matters where you end!

Dare to think differently. It's a small step with big consequences. Strive for the renewal of your mind. Bartimaeus heard the mood of the crowd change and he wondered what had happened. Someone told him that Jesus of Nazareth was passing by, and the blind beggar seized his moment. He began crying out, "Jesus, Son of David, have mercy on me!" His mind was able to embrace a new reality that helped him to perceive his circumstances differently. He realized that the power of God's Son was available to him. It is the power that changes dead wombs into fertile ones, straightens bent-over backs, dries up oozing wounds, and opens the eyes of the blind. He was not blind to the severity of his condition. He was able to see that Jesus had the ability to do something about it.

Bartimaeus heard that Jesus was passing by and he cried out. Two important terms to consider are that he "heard" and then he "cried out." He used what he had. He could not see, but he did not use blindness as an excuse not to use what he did possess. He used his ears, his mouth, his mind, and, most important, his faith. Despite his condition, he still had some tools available to help him get closer to Jesus.

Always use what is available, even if it looks like you don't have everything that you need. When you are handicapped in one area, don't use that as an excuse for not employing the other tools that you have. Just because you don't have an IQ of 150 doesn't mean you can't get through college. Just because you're not the prettiest or most handsome doesn't mean you won't have meaningful relationships in life.

When Bartimaeus heard that Jesus of Nazareth was near, he seized the moment. When he got up and had someone take him to the roadside that morning, he had no idea that Jesus would be passing by that day. It was just an ordinary day. But an opportunity passed his way and he took hold. Opportunity can be all around us, but often we don't latch on to the moment.

Bartimaeus shouted to get Jesus' attention. People told him to shut up. He didn't. Instead, he cried out more. Two Greek words for "cried" are *eboesen* ("to cry out") and *ekrasen*, meaning he escalated his efforts and cried outmore when they told him to shut up.

Sometimes people will see you moving earnestly toward the life Christ intended for you and they want to silence you. Some people can't handle your intentional desire to be better in this world. Bartimaeus was undaunted by the crowd's chastisement. He was willing to pay the price of their criticism for the chance to get close to Jesus. He was not living for someone else's approval. He shouted above the jeers and the stares. He would not allow people who had no vested interest in his quality of life to determine his future. He did not allow the crowd to intimidate him out of his blessing.

Someone will always be around to criticize you as you take steps toward being a better you. They may tell you to stop or to be silent or to just give up. Keep going, even in the face of opposition.

When you step out in faith, there will always be haters and detractors, but Jesus will raise up a crowd to assist you and encourage you to come closer to him. In his downtime, the prophet Elijah thought he was alone. But God basically told him, "I have seven thousand more prophets who won't bow down to Baal" (see 1 Kings 19:18).

With the encouragement he received, Bartimaeus moved closer to the Messiah with abandon. He threw off his cloak, which apparently was the only thing he owned. His moment of transformation had arrived, and he would no longer need his beggar's cloak.

In your incremental forward motion of intentional discipleship, remove useless clutter and debris from your mind and spiritual space. You do not want to trip over fear or doubt on your way to your better life in Christ Jesus.

You Can Be a Disciple in the Real World

The strategy presented in this book is both doable and effective for intentional discipleship that brings us closer to God and yields a life that is pleasing to God.

Strategizing is important, but so is implementation. The small-step approach stretches believers beyond their current limitations to expand and engage in Christlikeness in the real world and its demands. Real-world disciples can grow, thrive, and impact lives in meaningful ways, just as Jesus changed the lives of the Twelve who were his inner circle, the Samaritan woman, the hemorrhaging woman (see Mark 5:25–34), Zacchaeus the tax collector, and blind Bartimaeus.

Discipleship in the real world requires creativity and thoughtfulness that provide and promote opportunities for you to learn, grow, and share in ministries that challenge and invigorate, rather than consume and annihilate.

You now have a strategy to live in the fullness of your faith, trust Christ, and fulfill your quest to become more like him, as you engage in the personal and corporate experiences of ministry, discipleship, and worship.

Now is the time for you to take the continual steps toward intentional discipleship so you can be bold and be better! When you stay on the journey, your small steps of increased faithfulness will evolve into giant leaps of spiritual growth.

When life gets in the way during those times you lose your desire to take deliberate steps to follow God on purpose (connect, explore, share, give, participate), then pray, go to church, praise God, read your Bible. When you reluctantly and begrudgingly serve the Lord without gladness, that's the time to dig your heels of intention in deeper.

Jesus emphasizes the importance of perseverance in prayer

toward the end of his Sermon on the Mount (see Matthew 7:7–11). In most Bible translations, Jesus' admonition reads: "ask...seek...knock." Literally translated, however, the passage would read, "Keep on asking and it will be given to you; keep on seeking and you will find; keep on knocking and it will be opened to you" (see v. 7). All three verbs are present imperatives. We can't just ask and give up. We must keep on asking and then seeking and then knocking. Intentional discipleship necessitates perseverance that does not give up when times are challenging or when our circumstances do not change as quickly as we had hoped.

In John 10:10, Jesus gives his disciples encouragement: "I came that they may have life and have it abundantly" (ESV). Jesus came to expand the boundaries of our expectations. He came to blow up the potential for each of us.

Our connectedness to God is a blessed assurance that the thief cannot steal from us what God has given us. Strive to attain and maintain that connection with intention and receive the abundant life that Christ came to give all who desired it.

May this be your prayer: *"My calling to fulfill is to grow. May I reach through that growth to be a center of social and personal metamorphosis that endows people with the capacity to be recipients of God's redemptive grace through Jesus Christ our Lord. Then, through their transformation, may they become catalysts that change lives, churches, communities, and countries. The Lord being my helper!"*

Acknowledgments

The Big Deal of Taking Small Steps to Move Closer to God was conceived in my heart one morning in the quietness of the Chautauqua Institution in upstate New York when I was a guest preacher at the invitation of the Reverend Joan Brown Campbell. Just as the prophet Habakkuk wrote, the vision was for an appointed time and place, and this one came to pass in the Tenth Episcopal District of the African Methodist Episcopal Church. Preachers and church members embraced a process of incremental discipleship as the "10 percent challenge." I watched and prayed during their initial baby steps and until now, when the lessons learned are in your hands.

There is also a cadre of special people whose encouragement, kindness, prodding, and coaching have blessed my life and enlarged my ministry. They looked beyond title and position to pray for me in times of great strength and great concern. They have also been the iron that sharpens iron, as one person sharpens another (see Proverbs 27:17).

Thank you, Hachette Book Group, for publishing this body of lessons, experiences, struggles, and triumphs. I am profoundly grateful to Adrienne Ingrum, senior editor at Hachette, for her brains, talent, and dedication. I'm grateful for the

Acknowledgments

Reverend Olivia M. Cloud, who is an insightful editor, always going the extra mile. They were like Shiphrah and Puah on the birthing stool (see Exodus 1:15)—patient and coaxing.

I praise God continuously for my mother in the ministry, the Reverend Cecelia Williams Bryant, whose vibrant prophetic ministry embraces me. The Reverends Angelique Mason, Joni M. Russ, Barbara Green, and Tremecia Jones are the prevailing prayer warriors who provided me prayer support.

Special thanks to Delta Sigma Theta Sorority, Inc., and national president Dr. Paulette C. Walker, for allowing me to serve as your national chaplain.

There are the Tenth District presiding elders, office staff, and volunteers, including the Reverends Vashti Jasmine Murphy Saint Jean, Tyronda and Lish Burgess, Leo Griffin, and George Johnson, along with Mrs. Romella Jones and Mrs. Shon Lee, who are valuable colaborers in ministry.

My partner in life and ministry, Dr. Stanley McKenzie, supervisor of missions, Tenth Episcopal District, has lived with this vision since its embryonic stage. He has been a wise critic and coach, helping to make this journey together profound and fun. He has shared the blessings and burdens of ministry with me along with our adult children, a son-in-love, and a grandchild. Thanks also to my big brother Carl Edward Murphy Smith, whose unending ideas nurture me. And finally, to our third-born, Joi Marie Murphy McKenzie, a published author in her own right who continually pushes me to the edge of my crazy schedule to write, think, do, and be!

About the Author

Bishop Vashti Murphy McKenzie serves as the 117th elected and consecrated bishop of the African Methodist Episcopal Church. Her historic election in the year 2000 represented the first time in the over 213-year history of the AME Church that a woman had obtained the level of Episcopal office. Currently she is honored to serve as the presiding prelate of the Tenth Episcopal District, which includes the state of Texas. She previously served as the presiding bishop of the Thirteenth Episcopal District, Tennessee and Kentucky, and the Eighteenth Episcopal District in Southern Africa. In each district she initiated an innovative ministry, building three group homes for children orphaned by AIDS in Swaziland and creating Believe, Inc., a faith-based nonprofit to help resource local congregations and provide scholarships.

Huffington Post celebrated her as one of "Fifty Powerful Women Religious Leaders." She has also been at the top of the list of "Great African American Female Preachers" and is on the "Honor Roll of Great African American Preachers" by *Ebony* magazine.

Bishop McKenzie is the author of five books. The first two books, *Not Without a Struggle* and *Strength in the Struggle,* concern leadership and professional growth for women. She revised *Not Without a Struggle* in 2012, as it remains a staple at seminaries and schools of religion. *Journey to the Well* helps women seek new directions for personal growth and transformation by following in the footsteps of the biblical Samaritan woman. *Swapping Housewives* tells the stories of Rachel, Jacob, and Leah and shares the twenty-first-century implications for married and unmarried love. Bishop McKenzie edited *Those Sisters Can Preach!* in 2013, a collection of sermons from twenty-two of some of the most revered contemporary African-American preachers.